SIX LECTURES ON

Economic Growth

SIX LECTURES ON

Economic Growth

By Simon Kuznets

THE JOHNS HOPKINS UNIVERSITY

THE FREE PRESS OF GLENCOE, ILLINOIS

Copyright © 1959 by The Free Press, a Corporation

Printed in the United States of America

Library of Congress Catalog Card No. 59-13596

DESIGNED BY SIDNEY SOLOMON

Foreword

THESE LECTURES were presented at the Centro de Estudios Monetarios Latinoamericanos (CEMLA) in Mexico City, in July, 1958. In the six meetings, it proved possible to cover most, but not all, of the topics touched upon in the text below.

The lectures deal briefly with findings and hypotheses that warrant more detailed evidence and more rigorously formulated analysis. But I preferred to cover a wider scope rather than encumber the discussion with detailed data or with mathematical formulae, more appropriate to publications designed for reference.

The text is in essence a summary discussion of topics, many of which I have dealt with in greater detail in other papers.[1] But as in all attempts at a summary in a wide field, somewhat different emphases and new elements have been added.

Since my work on quantitative aspects of the economic

---

1. In addition to the three papers listed in the notes to Tables 1, 5, and 9, the following may be noted: (1) "Toward a Theory of Economic Growth," Robert Lekachman (ed.), *National Policy for Economic Welfare at Home and Abroad* (New York: Columbia University Bicentennial Conference, 1955), pp. 12-77 and 93-103; (2) "Economic Growth and Income Inequality," *The American Economic Review*, XLV, No. 1 (March, 1955), 1-28; (3) "Regional Economic Trends and Levels of Living," Philip M. Hauser (ed.), *Population and World Politics* (Glencoe, Ill.: The Free Press, 1958), pp. 79-117; (4) "Sur la Croissance Économique des Nations Modernes," *Économie Appliquée*, X, Nos. 2 and 3 (April and September, 1957), 211-259; (5) "Economic Growth of Small Nations," Alfred Bonné (ed.), *The Challenge of Development* (Jerusalem: Hebrew University, 1958), pp. 9-25.

growth of nations—the central topic here—is continuing, the lectures are in the nature of an interim progress report.

I am indebted to Mr. Javier Marquez, Director of CEMLA, for the opportunity to present the lectures; and to Miss Lillian Epstein for valuable assistance in preparing the tables and in editing the text. A Spanish edition was published by CEMLA in August, 1959, under the title, *Aspectos Cuantitavos del Desarrollo Económico.*

Simon Kuznets

Contents

[7]

Lecture V

Lecture VI

Tables

SIX LECTURES ON

Economic Growth

Lecture I

THE MEANING
AND MEASUREMENT
OF ECONOMIC GROWTH

ECONOMIC ACTIVITY is concerned with the provision of goods needed to satisfy human wants, individual and collective. Hence, economic growth of a firm, an industry, a nation, a region, means (whatever else it may imply) a sustained increase in the output of such goods. It must be an increase, if it is to represent growth rather than stagnation or decay. And the increase must be in the volume of product, the provision of which is, from the standpoint of society, the rationale for economic activity. Finally, the increase must be sustained over a period long enough to reflect more than a cyclical expansion, an unusually large harvest, a post-calamity recovery, or some other transient rise.

This definition is quite general: it covers the economic growth of Periclean Athens, Augustan Rome, medieval France, modern United States, and even India and Egypt in some centuries. Being so general, it is hardly useful as a preliminary guide to the topic of central interest to us here—the economic growth of nations in modern times, i.e., during the last one and one-half to two centuries. Modern economic growth of nations has two distinctive features: in *all* cases it involves a sustained and substantial rise in product per capita, and in *almost all cases* it involves a sustained and substantial rise in population. In the more distant past, economic growth meant in many cases a sustained rise in total population and in total product, but not in per capita product; moreover, the rates of rise were far more moderate than those of modern times. When there was a substantial rise in per capita product, it was usually a result of reduced population pressures following drastic declines in numbers. To repeat, the distinctive feature of modern economic growth is the frequent combination of high rates of growth of the total population and of per capita product, implying even higher rates of growth of total product.

The emphasis on a sustained and substantial rise in *per capita* product is particularly important because of its implications for the structure and conditions of modern economic growth. Given the structure of human wants, a cumulatively large rise in a country's per capita product necessarily means a shift in relative proportions of various goods demanded and used—and hence major changes in combinations of productive factors, in patterns of life, and in international relations. Furthermore, a rise in per capita product usually means an even larger rise in product per unit of labor input—since some of the extra product is ordinarily exchanged for more leisure, a concomitant of a higher standard of living. However, marked rises in product per labor unit, when population and therefore labor force are increasing, are usually possible only through major innovations, i.e., applications of new bodies of tested knowledge to the processes of economic production. Indeed, modern economic growth is, in substance, an application of the industrial system, i.e., a system of production based on increasing use of modern scientific knowledge. But this also means structural change as new industries appear and old industries recede in importance—which, in turn, calls for the capacity of society to absorb such changes; society must be able to accommodate itself to and adopt the successive innovations that raise per capita productivity. Thus the rise in per capita product is emphasized because of its implications—the structural changes that necessarily accompany it, and all that these changes imply because of their origin in technological innovations and because of their requirements in the way of society's adaptability to change.

The difficulties in measuring economic growth, supply of empirical data apart, lie precisely in this point: modern economic growth implies major structural changes and correspondingly large modifications in social and institutional conditions under which the greatly increased product per capita is attained. Yet for purposes of measurement, the changing components of the structure must be reduced to a common denominator; otherwise it would be impossible to compare the product of the economy of the United States with that of China, or the product of an advanced country today with its output a century ago before many of the goods and industries that loom so large today were known.

The numerous problems that arise in an attempt to reduce national products of differing composition, originating under different social conditions, to comparable aggregates that are divisible into additive parts, can scarcely be mentioned here, let alone discussed. I shall have to assume familiarity with the questions of scope (inclusion and exclusion), netness and grossness, and basis of valuation, that are usually treated in discussing conceptual problems in measurement of national product; and with the subdivisions by industry of origin, factor and type of income, type of use, domestic and foreign origin, etc., that yield the component classifications usually distinguished. It is important, however, to point out the major assumptions on the basis of which these thorny, and essentially insoluble, problems are usually resolved in actual measurement.

The basic assumption is the community of human nature in that the weights attached to various outputs, or productive factors, although taken from one or a few societies, have meaning for all or at least most of them. This is clearly a prerequisite for all comparisons over space or time. If we assumed that people today are radically different from their forebears of fifty to a hundred years ago, no meaningful comparisons over time could be made. Or if we assumed that the inhabitants of the United States and those of the U.S.S.R. are so different that food, clothing, etc., or labor and capital goods, mean quite different things to them, comparison of the national product of the two countries would be impossible—unless it referred to some exogenous base of valuation with no specified meaning in either country.

Secondly, in actual application, the sets of concepts and weights employed are those of one or a few economies, or of one or a few points in time. And the weights chosen are usually those of the more developed rather than the less developed economies, of the more recent point of time rather than the earlier. Thus, the translation in the international comparison made by the United Nations (used in some of the tables below) is to the purchasing power of the United States dollar, and the same was true of Colin Clark's "international unit" (until the third edition in 1957, when the "Oriental unit" was introduced). Likewise, in the measurement of changes over time, product is usually expressed in constant prices of recent years, not in prices of the past. There is a rationale for these choices, over and above the practical convenience of the greater availability of data for the advanced economies and for recent years. We evaluate economic growth from the vantage point of the higher levels already attained—both in looking back in time and in looking at the lower levels of less advanced economies: we live today and not in the past, and the less advanced economies aspire to the levels of the more advanced, not vice versa. In other words, the more advanced economies and the more recent times yield the *criteria* of economic growth.

Thirdly, it has generally been emphasized that the use of weights and concepts typical of advanced economies, or of recent decades, introduces a bias into comparisons that favors these more advanced units or more recent periods. This upward bias has been ascribed to the obvious danger of excluding from the measures non-market-bound activities that are proportionately much greater in less than in more advanced economies, and in earlier than in more recent decades; and to the fact that our measures do not make full allowance for the costs of the higher levels of output—greater costs of urban life, of accommodation to the job, etc.—which may be proportionately greater for advanced economies and for the more recent decades. There are also factors making for an opposite bias. Thus the use of recent price weights tends to yield a lower rate of growth, in so far as the goods that grow most rapidly are also those whose prices usually decline most. Likewise, the use of the price weights of the advanced countries tends to give many raw materials and simpler goods in the under-developed countries *higher* standing (relative to the complex manufacturing products) than they in fact have, and since the proportion of such goods is larger in these countries, there is an upward bias in valuation relative to that in the more advanced economies. One should not, therefore, jump to the conclusion that the common basis of valuation and treatment in international and inter-temporal comparisons produces a bias that favors *uniformly* the more advanced economy or the more recent period. Indeed, from the standpoint of the less advanced economy or the earlier decade, the present procedures may *under-estimate* the differences across space or the rate of growth over time.

Whatever the case, the conceptual and other difficulties of measurement do not justify the refusal to measure and the substitution of a cavalier treatment of uncontrolled impressions (even if embodied in apparently precise math-ematical models) for the strenuous task of empirical cor-roboration and testing. Despite the limitations resulting from a scarcity of basic, underlying data and from concepts that are outmoded because of a serious cultural lag, much can be learned by a determined scrutiny of the data—provided that one looks at them with significant questions in mind and is sufficiently familiar with the characteristics of both the data and the underlying processes. Whatever mistakes one may make in the process—and they will be many—can at least be corrected by others; cumulative improvement and learning are possible so long as the data are mobilized to serve as a basis of one set of generalizations and as a check on another.

THE HIGH RATES OF
MODERN ECONOMIC GROWTH

Table 1 brings together the rates of growth of population, per capita product, and total product (both in constant prices) for nineteen countries. These are all the countries, with population of no less than a million in recent years, for which the records cover a long period—at least four decades, and in most countries extending over half a century. Table 2 provides similar data for countries in Latin America, but the records cover a much shorter period— only twenty-five years. Since I am not well familiar with these estimates, I cannot place too much emphasis upon them in the analysis. My discussion will, therefore, be largely limited to the evidence of Table 1, with only passing references to the rest of the world.

The first point to be noted is that the records reflect the growth of countries, of national units. In theory, other units could be used—other area divisions, industries, groups of producers distinguished by their organizational characteristics (households, corporations, etc.), down to the individual firm. Indeed, since growth is an aspect of economic activity at large, the primary units engaged in such activity could be combined in various ways, and growth could be observed and analyzed for a wide variety of larger com-

Table 1—Recent Levels and Past Rates of Growth: Population, Product Per Capita, and Total Product; Selected Countries (with Long Period of Coverage)

COUNTRY	RECENT YEARS		RATES OF GROWTH			PER CENT CHANGE PER DECADE		
	Population Mid-1953 (millions) (1)	Product Per Capita 1952-54 (U.S. dollars) (2)	Initial Period (3)	Terminal Period (4)	Decades in Interval (5)	Population (6)	Product Per Capita (7)	Total Product (8)
1. United Kingdom[a]	50.6	780	1860-69	1949-53	8.65	8.0	12.5	21.5
2. Ireland and Eire[b]	2.9	410	1860-69	1949-53	8.65	-3.5	16.8	12.8
3. France	42.9	740	1841-50	1949-53	10.55	1.3	13.8	15.3
4. Germany[c]	49.0	510	1860-69	1950-54	8.75	10.1	15.1	27.4
5. Switzerland	4.9	1,010	1890-99	1949-53	5.65	7.7	15.3	24.4
6. Netherlands	10.5	500	1900-1908	1950-54	4.8	14.3	9.0	24.6
7. Denmark[d]	4.4	750	1870-78	1950-54	7.8	10.9	16.7	29.4
8. Norway[e]	3.4	740	1900-1908	1950-54	4.8	8.2	23.4	33.5
9. Sweden[f]	7.2	950	1861-68	1950-54	8.75	6.6	27.6	36.0
10. Italy	47.6	310	1862-68	1950-54	8.7	6.9	10.4	18.0
11. Spain	28.5[h]	250[i]	1906-13	1949-53	4.15	8.8	5.6	14.9
12. Hungary	9.2[i]	269[i]	1899-1901	1949	4.9	6.2	8.7	15.5
13. Russia and U.S.S.R.[g]	207.0[j]	500[j]	1870	1954	8.4	13.4	15.4	31.0
14. United States	159.6	1,870	1869-78	1950-54	7.85	17.4	20.3	41.2
15. Canada[k]	14.8	1,310	1870-79	1950-54	7.75	18.3	19.3	41.3
16. Union of South Africa	13.2	300	1911/12	1949/50-1952/53	3.95	20.9	23.8	49.7
17. Japan	86.7	190	1878-87	1950-54	6.95	12.7	26.3	42.3
18. Australia	8.8	950	1898-1903	1949/50-1953/54	5.1	17.2	9.5	28.4
19. New Zealand	2.0	1,000	1901	1949/50-1953/54	5.025	18.7	11.8	32.7

Unless otherwise indicated, the entries in columns 1 and 2 are from "Per Capita National Product of Fifty-Five Countries: 1952-1954," United Nations, *Statistical Papers, Series E*, No. 4 (New York, 1957); and the entries in columns 3-8, from Simon Kuznets, "Quantitative Aspects of the Economic Growth of Nations: I. Levels and Variability of Rates of Growth," *Economic Development and Cultural Change*, Vol. V, No. 1 (October, 1956), particularly Tables 1 and 2.

The interval in column 5 is calculated from the mid-point of the initial period to the mid-point of the terminal period. All rates of growth in columns 7 and 8 are for net national product in constant prices, unless otherwise indicated.

a. Excluding southern Ireland.

b. The entries for 1952-54 are for Eire. The rates of change in columns 6-8 are weighted averages of the rates for Ireland for 1860-69 to 1904-13 (weight 4.4) and for Eire for 1911 to 1949-53 (weight 4).

c. The entries for 1952-54 are for West Germany. The rates of change in columns 6-8 are weighted averages of the rates for the pre-World War I territory for 1860-69 to 1905-14 (weight 4.5); for the 1925 territory for 1913 to 1935-41 (weight 2.5); and for West Germany for 1936 to 1950-54 (weight 1.6).

d. The rates in columns 7 and 8 are for net domestic product. A correction of about 5 per cent was made for inclusion of the area of North Schleswig in 1920 and later years.

e. The rates in columns 7 and 8 are for gross national product.

f. The rates in columns 7 and 8 are for gross domestic product.

g. The rates in columns 6-8 are weighted averages of the rates for European Russia for 1870-1913 (weight 4.3) and for the U.S.S.R. for 1913-54 (weight 4.1). The national product in columns 7 and 8 excludes personal and government services.

h. The population total is from the United Nations *Demographic Yearbook*, 1954; per capita product is a crude estimate based on the relation in 1948 to the comparable figure for Italy, given in W. S. and E. S. Woytinsky, *World Population and Production* (Twentieth Century Fund, 1953), Table 186, pp. 392-93, and applied to the figure for Italy in column 2.

i. The entry is for 1949; from "National and Per Capita Incomes, Seventy Countries—1949," United Nations, *Statistical Papers, Series E*, No. 1 (New York, 1950).

j. The population total is from Colin Clark, *Conditions of Economic Progress* (3rd ed.; London, 1957), Table XXVI, p. 250. Figures in that table yield a per capita net national product (in I.U.'s) of about 300, compared with 1,128 for the United States for 1952 (*ibid.*, Table XI, p. 193). This suggests a figure of roughly 500 United States dollars.

k. The rates in columns 7 and 8 are for gross national product.

Table 2—Recent Levels and Past Rates of Growth: Population, Product Per Capita, and Total Product; Latin America

DATA AND SOURCES	Argentina (1)	Brazil (2)	Chile (3)	Colombia (4)	Mexico (5)	Other Latin American Countries (6)
United Nations Data						
1. Population, mid-1953, millions	18.4	55.8	6.4	12.1	28.1	36.7[a]
2. Product per capita at factor cost, average 1952-54, U. S. dollars	460	230	360	250	220	247[a]
ECLA Data						
3. Population, 1950-54, millions	18.0	54.5	6.3	11.9	27.3	44.2
4. Gross domestic product per capita, 1950-54, U. S. dollars at 1950 prices	557	208	318	228	221	252
Rates of Change Per Decade, 1925-29 to 1950-54						
5. Population	21.9	24.4	17.6	23.5	24.7	16.4
6. Gross domestic product per capita	4.4	15.8	15.5	22.6	43.2	28.7
7. Total gross domestic product	27.3	44.2	35.7	51.4	78.4	49.9

The entries in lines 1 and 2 are from United Nations, *Statistical Papers, Series E*, No. 4 (New York, 1957). The product figures are net national product at factor cost. The population figures in lines 3 and 5, except those for "other Latin American countries," are based upon the annual estimates of the United Nations Statistical Office. The latter are the difference between the total for Latin America and the sum of the estimates for the individual countries shown. Total population for Latin America and all product figures other than those in lines 1 and 2 are based upon estimates by the Economic Commission for Latin America, as summarized by Alexander Ganz in "Problems and Uses of National Wealth Estimates in Latin America," a paper submitted to the De Pietersberg Conference of the International Association for Research in Income and Wealth, August, 1957. The product figures are gross domestic product at market prices.

a. The total or weighted average for the following countries shown separately in the source: Cuba, Dominican Republic, Ecuador, Guatemala, Honduras, Jamaica, Panama, Paraguay, Peru, Puerto Rico, and Venezuela, posite units. It is no accident that we begin with the nation-state as the unit for observing economic growth, nor is it to be explained merely by the way the data are most easily available. Nations are the foci of differences and decisions: the historical past of each is a distinctive complex and sets specific conditions for its economic growth, and the organization of each into a political community is of major importance in permitting secular decisions conducive (or inimical) to economic growth. This does not mean that we should not distinguish industries, or regions, or groups of economic organizations, within each nation; or combine nations into larger and more comprehensive complexes. Yet the nation is the dominant unit of observation and analysis, and has been such in much of the history of economics as an intellectual discipline (*vide* its original name of *political* economy). However, like any other limiting choice, the emphasis on the nation-state as the unit of observation and analysis has its limiting consequences which we shall have to bear in mind when we look at the results.

The sample in Table 1 is confined largely to what we now designate economically developed countries, with a few exceptions such as Spain, Ireland, and Hungary, and the intermediate case of Italy. Whatever generalizations we derive from it are thus based on observations relating to a small part of the world—a sample of roughly twenty states out of more than eighty; of less than 700 million people out of a world population of over 2.5 billion. More important, Table 1 includes all the developed countries of the world with few exceptions (e.g., Belgium), and its scope, already somewhat exaggerated by the inclusion of units that cannot be considered economically advanced, indicates the limits of the spread of the industrial system. The fact of the matter is that in the well over one and one-half centuries since the industrial revolution in Great Britain, the industrial system has spread to only a limited part of the world and includes only about a quarter of the world population. The technological and social changes resulting from the emergence and evolution of the industrial system did, of course, have a wider impact, but that impact did not advance the economic performance of the rest of the world to levels anywhere near those for most of the countries in Table 1.

The one outstanding characteristic of modern economic growth, where we can observe it, is the high rate of increase. For population, except in Ireland and France, the rate of increase ranges from 6 to over 20 per cent per decade. For per capita income, except in Spain and Hungary, the rate ranges from close to 10 to well over 20 per cent per decade. As a result, the rate of increase in total product is even higher—never falling below 10 per cent per decade and ranging in most cases from 15 to over 40 per cent.

Since high and low are relative terms, the base of reference must be specified. One way of doing so is to consider what cumulated rates mean over a long period. A rate of increase of 10 per cent per decade, if sustained over a century, means a rise to 2.6 times the initial value; over two centuries, a rise to 6.7 times the initial value. A rate of increase of 15 per cent per decade over a century cumulates to a rise to 4.0 times the original value; over two centuries, to over 16 times the original value. A rate of increase of 20 per cent per decade means a rise over a century to 6.2 times the initial value; over two centuries, to over 38 times the initial value. Yet in six of the nineteen countries listed in Table 1 (Norway, Sweden, United States, Canada, Union of South Africa, and Japan) per capita income increased close to, or well over, 20 per cent per decade; and in four of these countries the records cover a period not far short of a century. Clearly, the rates are high in the sense that their cumulation over a century or two means rises that stagger the imagination.

The rates of increase, particularly in per capita income, are also high in that, judging by a variety of evidence, they could not have prevailed over many decades in most of the world, nor could they have prevailed over a very long period in any country no matter how highly developed it is today. The first part of this inference can be easily corroborated if we recognize that in much of the world, as indicated by a variety of international comparisons, *present* levels of per capita income are relatively low. If we use per capita national product estimates for 1952-54 (or some earlier year in a few cases) prepared by the United Nations, and set the maximum income for underdeveloped countries at roughly $100 (in purchasing power of 1952-54), most of the populous countries of Asia (China, India, Pakistan, Indonesia, Burma, South Korea, Thailand) and many in Africa—close to half of the world population—would fall within this group. In these countries, and the many others with per capita incomes only slightly above $100, growth in per capita income over past decades could not have been substantial. Extrapolation backward of rates of increase like those in Table 1 would yield impossible levels in earlier times, impossible because life could not have been maintained at such low levels. Then, too, we have some direct evidence on the presently underdeveloped countries, e.g., India and Egypt, showing that over the last five decades, indeed since the beginning of the century, there was scarcely any rise in real per capita income.

The second part of the inference, viz., that the rates of rise in per capita income for the developed countries could not have prevailed over very long periods, can be demonstrated by extrapolating the rates in Table 1 back and observing that low levels are reached too rapidly to be historically true. This is the purpose of Table 3, in which we extrapolate back from the 1952-54 levels of per capita income by rates of growth shown in Tables 1 and 2. If we assume that a per capita income of $100 in 1952-54 prices (about half the level for Japan) is about rock bottom for the northern and western countries, extrapolation would bring us to this level in most of the presently developed countries (except Australia and New Zealand) by the late eighteenth, early nineteenth, or even the middle of the nineteenth century. If the extrapolation represented reality, it would mean that: (a) the initial levels of per capita income, at the dates shown in column 6, were for the presently developed countries as low as $100 in 1952-54 prices; (b) there could not have been any sustained growth in per capita income before those dates. We know that neither implication is true. Certainly per capita income in the United Kingdom in 1779 and in the United States in 1795 was not that low; and certainly growth in per capita income in both countries had been substantial before these dates. It follows that the rates of growth shown in Tables 1 and 2 are exceptionally high in the sense that they could not have persisted over really long periods in the past. Regardless of whether we can envisage continuation of such rates in the future, the records of the past tell us that against the perspective of many centuries of human history, the rates of growth of both population and per capita income (and

Table 3—Regression to Assumed Low Values of Income Per Capita, Number of Decades and Dates; Selected Countries in Tables 1 and 2

COUNTRY	Decades Required for Regression to Per Capita Income (in 1952-54 U. S. dollars) of:				Dates at Which the Country Would Reach the Per Capita Income of:			
	200	100	50	25	200	100	50	25
	(1)	(2)	(3)	(4)	(5)	(6)	(7)	(8)
1. United Kingdom	11.6	17.4	23.3	29.2	1837	1779	1720	1661
2. Ireland and Eire	4.6	9.1	13.5	18.0	1907	1862	1818	1773
3. France	10.1	15.5	20.8	26.2	1852	1798	1745	1691
4. Germany	6.7	11.6	16.5	21.4	1886	1837	1788	1739
5. Switzerland	11.4	16.2	21.1	26.0	1839	1791	1742	1693
6. Netherlands	10.6	18.7	26.7	34.8	1847	1766	1686	1605
7. Denmark	8.6	13.0	17.5	22.0	1867	1823	1778	1733
8. Norway	6.2	9.5	12.8	16.1	1891	1858	1825	1792
9. Sweden	6.4	9.2	12.1	14.9	1889	1861	1832	1804
10. Italy	4.4	11.4	18.4	25.4	1909	1837	1769	1699
11. Russia and U.S.S.R.	6.4	11.2	16.1	20.9	1889	1841	1792	1744
12. United States	12.1	15.8	19.6	23.3	1832	1795	1757	1720
13. Canada	10.7	14.6	18.5	22.4	1846	1807	1768	1729
14. Union of South Africa	1.9	5.1	8.4	11.6	1934	1902	1869	1837
15. Japan	−0.2	2.7	5.7	8.7	1955	1926	1896	1866
16. Australia	17.2	24.8	32.4	40.1	1781	1705	1629	1552
17. New Zealand	14.4	20.6	26.9	33.1	1809	1747	1684	1622
18. Brazil	1.0	5.7	10.4	15.1	1943	1896	1849	1802
19. Chile	4.1	8.9	13.7	18.5	1912	1864	1816	1768
20. Colombia	1.1	4.5	7.9	11.3	1942	1908	1874	1840
21. Mexico	0.3	2.2	4.1	6.1	1950	1931	1912	1892
22. Other Latin American countries	0.8	3.6	6.3	9.1	1945	1917	1890	1862

This calculation accepts the levels of per capita income for 1952-54 given in Table 1, column 2; and Table 2, line 2. Using the rates of growth (per decade) in per capita income, in Table 1, column 7, and Table 2, line 6, it derives the number of decades by which a regression (growth backward) from the 1952-54 levels would yield the low levels of per capita income in columns 1-4.

With the number of decades given, the dates in columns 5-8 are obtained by subtracting the years involved from 1953 (the mid-point of the 1952-54 period).

hence of total income) in the recent past were unusually high.

The extremely high rate of modern growth in population, suggesting what demographers often refer to as a "population explosion," has been observed and known for some time; nor is there anything new about the conspicuously high rate of modern growth in income per capita. While these facts have become increasingly known and accepted, some of their implications are not so well recognized. It is to these implications that we now turn.

Lecture II

THE NECESSARY CONDITION

As ALREADY NOTED, sustained high rates of growth of per capita income meant, in the decades covered by our estimates, even higher rates of growth in product per man-hour; when population also grew rapidly, this meant major changes in the production functions that could not have occurred except for continuous innovations—particularly for countries where extensive expansion was impossible. Innovation is a new application of either old or new knowledge to production processes (production defined broadly); since old knowledge, in a form ready for extensive application, is limited, a continuous and large rise in product per unit of labor is possible only with major additions of *new* technological and related knowledge. Continuous technological progress and, underlying it, a series of new scientific discoveries are the necessary condition for the high rate of modern growth in per capita income combined with a substantial rate of growth in population. As evidence, we need only note the industries that loom large in an advanced economy: many in the electrical, internal combustion, and chemical fields were entirely unknown a hundred years ago, and even the older industries are permeated by processes whose origin lies in relatively recent scientific discoveries.

In these days it is hardly necessary to emphasize that science is the base of modern technology, and that modern technology is in turn the base of modern economic growth. Without the emergence and development of modern science and science-based technology, neither economic production nor population could have grown at the high rates indicated for the last century to century and a half in the developed countries. True, growth of tested knowledge, both scientific generalization and empirical information, and of modern technology based on it, were necessary, not sufficient conditions: knowledge in itself does not suffice, for reasons some of which will be noted below. Yet the growth of science and technological knowledge has distinct patterns of its own; difficult as it is to discern them (particularly for a mere economist), some attempt should be made to do so, for they are relevant to the pattern, intra- or international, that modern economic growth exhibits.

In attempting to trace these patterns we may distinguish the following: a scientific discovery—an addition to knowledge, ranging from a minor item like the formula for a new organic compound to a major principle like that relating matter and energy; an invention—a tested combination of already existing knowledge to a useful end; an innovation—an initial and significant application of an invention, whether technological or social, to economic production; an improvement—a minor beneficial change in a known invention or process in the course of its application; and finally, the spread of an innovation, usually accompanied by improvements, either through extensive imitation or internal growth. While these can be seen as successive phases—from discovery to invention to innovation to improvement to spread—there is also a feed-back effect. The spread of innovations may favor further inventions, and the latter may stimulate further discovery.

Within this complex, two characteristics relevant to the problem of economic growth may be suggested. First, there is a bottleneck relationship between the successive phases—from the scientific discovery to the spread of an innovation. Each scientific discovery is potentially a base for a wide variety of inventions (which is one major reason why discoveries are not patentable), but not all these possible inventions are produced. Each invention is a candidate for an innovation, but only a small proportion of inventions is adopted. Each innovation is a candidate for widespread use, but only a limited proportion is extensively used and can then be characterized as major innovations. The factors that determine the choice of inventions made, among those possible with the given stock of scientific discoveries; of innovations made, among all the inventions that clamor for application; and among those, of major innovations, are diverse and still little known. But at the link where innovations transform new technological knowledge into production reality, three factors are obviously important: (a) Many major inventions, if they are to become successful innovations, demand heavy capital investment—both in material goods and in the training of the labor force. Material capital is necessary to channel properly the new power in its application to intricate ends, and an educated and skilled labor force is indispensable in operating complex machinery and production processes. (b) Innovations, by definition, represent something new and require entrepreneurial talents and skills to overcome a series of unexpected obstacles. (c) Much depends upon the responsiveness of the would-be users of the new products or processes who are the final judges of the potential technological changes to be adopted for widespread use and hence for mass production. All these requirements combined with the *necessary* condition of increased technological knowledge constitute the *sufficient* condition for modern economic growth.

Second, there is a tendency for scientific discovery, invention, and innovation to be concentrated at any given time in a few fields—rather than be evenly distributed among all. In the late eighteenth and early nineteenth centuries, it was the iron, stationary steam, and the cotton textile industries that constituted the focus of much invention and innovation. In the late nineteenth century emphasis was put upon electric power and communication, and then the internal combustion engine. In the mid-twentieth century emphasis is being put upon atomic energy, with the steam era well in the past and the electricity era coming to an end as a field for major discovery, invention, or innovation. There are two reasons for such shifts in the focus of discovery, invention, and innovation. First, the available intellectual and material resources are never sufficient for the pursuit of new knowledge, invention, or innovation in all possible fields with equal vigor; some choice, conscious or unconscious, of the more promising areas must be made. Second, at any given time only a few areas are *most* promising: the potential of further invention and innovation in the older areas is limited by earlier progress and growth, and some very new areas may not yet be ready for successful invention and innovation.

An important consequence for the pattern of economic growth follows. This shift of emphasis from one area within the productive system to another in addition to knowledge, new technology, and innovation means changes in the identity of the new and rapidly growing industries. By the same token, there is a tendency toward retardation in the rate of growth of older industries, as the economic effects of technical progress and innovation within them slacken and as they feel increasingly the competition of the newer industries for limited resources. To put it differently, a sustained high rate of growth depends upon a continuous emergence of new inventions and innovations, providing the bases for new industries whose high rates of growth compensate for the inevitable slowing down in the rate of invention and innovation, and upon the economic effects of both, which retard the rates of growth of the older industries. A high rate of over-all growth in an economy is thus necessarily accompanied by considerable shifting in relative importance among industries, as the old decline and the new increase in relative weight in the nation's output.

Another aspect of the interrelation of science, technology, and economic growth may be noted. In the late eighteenth and early nineteenth centuries, before some of the wide potentialities of scientific discovery and science-based technology became evident, there was a general tendency to assume a fairly narrow limit to the effects of technological change in offsetting increasing scarcity of irreproducible natural resources. One inference based on this view was that as a country develops economically, it must rely increasingly upon the natural resources of the less advanced countries. It would thus help spread the beneficial effects of modern economic growth elsewhere, since reliance upon supplies from the outside naturally means a *quid pro quo* in the way of industrial goods, capital, etc. The emphasis above on the availability of a much greater stock of knowledge than is in fact utilized in innovations, implies a fatal qualification upon this view, which connected the limited effects of technological change with the export of modern economic growth to the rest of the world. While economic growth in developed countries does lead to greater demand for raw materials from the rest of the world, it seems unlikely that investment opportunities for domestic savings in developed countries will be limited by the extreme costliness caused by scarcity of land or other natural resources under conditions of limited technological change. On the contrary, it may well be that the continuous growth in the rate of scientific discovery and potential technological change will provide *increasing* opportunities for domestic investment of the capital funds of the developed countries—leaving only enough capital exports to assure the supply of raw materials for the capital-exporters' domestic economy. To put it differently, the change in the rate of scientific discovery and potentially new technological development should lead to a careful and critical reconsideration of the nineteenth century notion that the limitations of natural resources in the more advanced countries automatically make for the spread of the industrial system to the rest of the world—as an inevitable sequence from raw materials to industrial products; from capital im-

port by the less developed countries for the expansion
of raw material production, to capital import for industrialization.

THE TIME PATTERN OF GROWTH

Do science-based technology and invention, as a necessary condition of modern economic growth, operating
within the limitations indicated above, set a time pattern
of growth, once a nation enters upon modern economic
development? By time pattern of growth we mean some
order in the sequence of rates of increase. Do the rates
rise, are they constant, or do they decline? And are there
any reasons to expect a systematic pattern?

The answer may well differ for various components
of a nation's economy, e.g., for population and for per
capita product; or for nations with different antecedents,
e.g., for old and settled countries like Great Britain and
Germany, and for young and "empty" countries with
room for expansion like the United States. Nevertheless,
some elements of general order can be suggested, and
these are important for our interpretation of secular trends
in those measures of economic growth that we have.

One element of order is clearly indicated by what has
already been said. The spread of the industrial system,
based on the additions to useful knowledge made since
the eighteenth century, meant much higher rates of growth
of population, per capita product, and total product, than
before. At some period in the transition from pre-modern

conditions to modern economic growth, therefore, there must have been a shift from lower to higher rates of growth. Since such shifts are rarely, if ever, sudden, there must have been a substantial period, extending over several decades, during which the rate of growth was accelerated, i.e., the rate of increase was rising.

Acceleration in the rate of growth of population occurs largely because new technology has the most immediate effect on death rates; birth rates are affected only with considerable lag, after the concomitant processes of urbanization, rising standard of living, and smaller family patterns begin to exercise their influence. Once the crude death rate is low, further absolute decline is limited; but no such limits are imposed on the crude birth rates. The later stages of modern economic growth in a country are likely, therefore, to be accompanied by a falling rate of natural increase, i.e., the excess of births over deaths as a percentage of total population. For simplicity's sake, we are disregarding international migration which may mitigate acceleration and retardation in some countries and exaggerate them in others. With this simplification, the time pattern of modern population growth emerges as a long curve, beginning with rising rates of growth, followed by a period of relatively constant rates, then followed by a period of retardation—all taking place in some timing relation, not yet clearly known, to the long-term growth of per capita and total product.

There are two important exceptions to, and one important implication in, this general pattern. The first exception occurs in the young and "empty" country, usually an overseas offshoot of western Europe, like the United States, Canada, Australia, and New Zealand. These

countries may not go through the early phase of acceleration in the percentage rates of growth of population,
since even their pre-modern rates of increase are quite
high and since the birth rates may decline even before
industrialization (as happened in the United States). The
second exception is the acceleration of population growth
in recent times in many less developed countries well before industrialization and modern economic growth begin: the spread of modern technology for lowering death
rates is far easier and faster than that of modern technology for increasing productivity.

The implication referred to above is obvious. If modern technology has the *early* effect of accelerating the rate
of growth in population, of producing what demographers
call "population swarming," the problem of a significant
and sustained rise in per capita income becomes all the
more difficult. For what is then required is not merely
an increase in product commensurate with the increase
in population, but a much greater rise sufficient to lift
the level of per capita income in order to provide a basis
for further sustained growth.

In such cases in the past when income per capita grew
at high rates, there must also have been acceleration over
the preceding decades. It would be helpful to know the
timing of the acceleration in growth of per capita income
relative to that in population, but our data do not reach
out into this period for enough countries to permit even
a rough general statement—except to suggest that the
acceleration in the rate of growth of per capita income
begins after that in the rate of natural increase of population.

The intriguing question is whether we should expect

the rate of growth in per capita income to fall after a while, from whatever high levels it may have reached at the end of the acceleration phase. Difficult as it is to imagine unlimited growth in any social process, there are no inherently *compelling* reasons for the rate of growth of per capita product to decline. In the light of our earlier discussion, technological and other limitations on the *supply* side can hardly be viewed as an important factor. The major reason would therefore lie on the demand side. A long-term rise in real income per capita would make leisure an increasingly preferred good, as is clearly evidenced by the marked reduction in the working week in freely organized, non-authoritarian advanced countries. One could argue that after a high level of per capita income is attained, the pressure on the demand side for further increases is likely to slacken. If so, there would eventually be retardation in the rate of growth of per capita income, but it would come much later than that in the rate of growth of population.

The time pattern of growth in total product is obviously a compound of those in growth of population and per capita product. Acceleration in the rate of growth of population, provided the rate of growth of per capita product does not decline, would necessarily produce acceleration in the rate of growth of total product; and the latter would be further accelerated when the growth in per capita product quickens. When both population and per capita product stabilize at a constant rate of growth, total product will also grow at a constant rate. When retardation in the rate of population growth begins, the growth of total product will be retarded, *unless* the rate of growth of per capita product begins at that point to accelerate—

which is highly unlikely. Thus one may expect a long secular swing in the rate of growth of total product, its phases of acceleration, constancy, and retardation falling, with respect to timing, between those for population and per capita product.

Before we consider the general implication of these time patterns, the evidence in Table 4 should be noted. Here we distinguish two sub-periods for those countries with relatively long records. Unfortunately, there are only eleven such countries, and even for some of these the value of the evidence is reduced by breaks in historical continuity and by the wide margins of error in the estimates for the early decades. In regard to population, if we exclude Ireland as the exceptional case, we find a retardation in the rate of growth, i.e., a lower rate in the second than in the first sub-period. The finding for Canada can be explained largely in terms of immigration, and that for Japan may not be significant because of deficiencies in population statistics for the early period. Regarding per capita product, we also find evidence of slowing down in the rate of growth, with the conspicuous exception of the U.S.S.R. and Italy whose industrialization occurs rather late, and of Sweden which managed to maintain its exceedingly high rate of growth of per capita income. The rates of growth in total product naturally reflect those just noted: in the majority of countries retardation is observed. Thus the evidence, on the whole, supports the notion of the time pattern suggested above —although it covers primarily the constant and downward phases of the pattern and does not reach sufficiently far back (except for the U.S.S.R. and Italy) to cover the acceleration phase.

Table 4—Rates of Growth of Population, Product Per Capita, and Total Product; Two Intervals within the Long Period; Selected Countries

COUNTRY	MIDDLE PERIOD	NUMBER OF DECADES		PER CENT CHANGE PER DECADE					
				Population		Product Per Capita		Total Product	
		Interval I	Interval II	Interval I	Interval II	Interval I	Interval II	Interval I	Interval II
	(1)	(2)	(3)	(4)	(5)	(6)	(7)	(8)	(9)
1. United Kingdom	1905-14	4.5	4.15	11.1	4.8	12.5	12.5	25.0	17.9
2. Ireland and Eire[a]	1904-13	4.4	4.0	-5.4	-1.4	17.9	15.7	11.6	14.2
3. France	1901-10	6.0	4.55	1.9	0.6	16.3	10.4	18.6	11.1
4. Germany[b]	1905-14	4.5	3.9	11.5	8.6	21.6	8.4	35.6	18.9
5. Denmark	1904-13	3.45	4.35	11.3	11.0	19.3	14.7	32.7	27.3
6. Sweden	1904-13	4.4	4.35	6.8	6.4	26.2	28.9	34.8	37.2
7. Italy	1904-13	4.35	4.35	7.0	6.7	8.1	12.7	15.7	20.3
8. Russia and U.S.S.R.[c]	1913	4.3	4.1	15.7	11.1	10.4	21.0	27.7	34.4
9. United States	1904-13	3.5	4.35	22.3	13.7	27.5	14.7	56.0	30.4
10. Canada	1905-14	3.5	4.25	17.8	18.8	24.7	15.0	47.1	36.6
11. Japan	1908-17	3.0	3.95	12.0	13.3	32.2	22.0	47.9	38.2
11a. Japan[d]		3.0	3.0	12.0	12.8	32.2	37.2	47.9	54.7

The data are from the source cited for Table 1, columns 6-8. Here we used Table 2 and the detailed appendix tables of the original source. In general, the aim was to divide the long period fairly equally, but in most cases the division line is just before World War I. The period given in column 1 is the terminal period of the first interval and the initial period of the second interval. The entries in column 1, together with those in Table 1, columns 3 and 4, give the distribution of the total time span into the two intervals. For other notes on the series for the various countries, see Table 1.

a. The first interval runs from 1860-69 to 1904-13, and relates to all Ireland. The second interval runs from 1911 to 1949-53, and relates to Eire proper.

b. The first interval runs from 1860-69 to 1905-14 and relates to the territory of the Reich before 1913. The rates for the second interval are weighted averages of the rates for 1913 to 1935-41 for the post-Versailles territory (weight 2.5); and for 1936 to 1950-54 for West Germany (weight 1.6).

c. The first interval is for the period 1870-1913, and relates to the U.S.S.R. (interwar territory). The second interval is for the period 1913-1954, and relates to pre-World War I European Russia. The rates for 1913 to 1935-41 for the post-Versailles territory...

d. In the second grouping of intervals for Japan, the first interval runs from 1878-87 to 1908-17; the second interval runs from 1903-12 to 1933-42. The 1933-42 decade shows the highest per capita income for the period from 1878-87 to 1950-54.

The general implication of such a pattern can be clearly perceived if we assume that countries do not enter upon modern economic growth simultaneously. On this premise, their phases of acceleration, of constant high rates, and of retardation all occur at different times. The result of such differences in timing, combined with the nature of the pattern, can be seen most clearly if we assume as an initial simplification that the rates, duration of phases, and extent of acceleration and retardation are identical for all countries. On this assumption, differences in timing of entry of the various countries upon modern economic growth mean correlative differences in the rates of growth of population, per capita, and total product. Countries that start later than others soon shift from a position lagging behind the early entrants into a position where their rates of growth are distinctly higher than those of the early entrants which meanwhile may have entered the retardation phase. Such shifts among countries in relative rates of growth of population and product are pregnant with political shifts and strains. Obviously, greater knowledge about the time patterns of economic growth, the duration of the phases, and the rates involved, would shed light on the effects that different times of entry into modern economic growth have on the relative economic position of nations; hence also, on the stresses and strains that shifts in economic position may engender.

Lecture III

FINDINGS ON
INDUSTRIAL STRUCTURE
OF LABOR FORCE
AND NATIONAL PRODUCT

THE ASSOCIATION between industrial structure and economic growth can be studied in two ways. First, employing some available index of economic growth such as national income per capita, we can, for a recent period, array the countries by their income per capita, and observe the differences in the industrial structure of labor force and of national income among countries. The cross-section correlation between income per capita and industrial structure thus revealed would at least suggest what may be expected in most countries in the course of modern economic growth. The second, and more direct, approach is to study the long-term records for those countries for which we have the data, and ascertain the changes in industrial structure that actually occurred in the course of their economic growth.

Tables 5, 6, and 7 summarize the statistical findings by both approaches. In Table 5, countries are classified into seven groups by per capita income in 1949 or in 1952-54, in U.S. dollars, with countries with the highest per capita in group I and those with the lowest in group VII. (Per capita income is one of several measures of the economic level of a country that could be used—national product per worker, output of consumer goods per consumer unit, and so on; but since they are all closely interrelated, they would yield rather similar groupings of countries.) Then for each country we calculated, for a post-World War II period, usually a quinquennium in the 1950's, the percentage shares in the labor force (excluding unpaid family labor) and in national income (or some variant of the latter) of the major sectors: agriculture and related industries, such as forestry and fishing (A sector); mining, manufacturing, and construction (M sector); and all other activities (S sector), including such divisions as transport and communication (T division); trade, banking, and other finance (C division); and the remaining service activities, ranging from professional, personal, and business to government (OS division). Unweighted arithmetic means of these percentage shares were calculated for each group, each country being taken as a unit equivalent to others, regardless of the size of its population, territory, etc. In general, only countries with more than one million inhabitants in recent years were included.

In Tables 6 and 7 we summarize long-term changes in industrial structure for the much smaller number of countries for which such records can be found. Here labor force includes unpaid family labor (no other data are easily available over long periods) but the results would not be much different for labor force excluding this component. The shares in national product are for volumes in current prices, as is the case in Table 5.

Table 5—Industrial Structure of Labor Force and of National Product; Countries Grouped by Product Per Capita (Based on Estimates in Current Prices, Averages for Post-World War II Years)

Sectors in Distribution of Labor Force and Income	Groups of Countries by Product Per Capita							Wider Groups		
	I (1)	II (2)	III (3)	IV (4)	V (5)	VI (6)	VII (7)	I+II (8)	III+IV (9)	V+VI+VII (10)
I DISTRIBUTION OF LABOR FORCE (EXCL. UNPAID FAMILY LABOR)										
Distribution among A, M, and S										
1. Number of countries	7	6	5	5	4	7	4	13	10	15
Average Percentage Share of										
2. A sector	14.4	23.4	27.9	51.1	49.7	57.5	61.2	18.6	39.5	56.4
3. M sector	40.3	34.8	30.3	20.7	22.0	16.4	15.1	37.8	25.5	17.6
4. S sector	45.3	41.7	41.8	28.2	28.3	26.1	23.7	43.6	35.0	26.1
Distribution of S Sector										
5. Number of countries	7	6	5	5	4	7	4	13	10	15
Average Percentage Share of										
6. T division	8.6	7.6	6.4	4.0	4.0	3.5	2.6	8.1	5.2	3.4
7. C division	15.1	11.4	11.5	8.0	8.2	6.1	5.8	13.4	9.7	6.5
8. T+C division	23.7	18.9	17.8	12.0	12.1	9.6	8.3	21.5	14.9	9.9
9. OS division	21.7	22.8	24.0	16.2	16.2	16.6	15.3	22.2	20.1	16.1
II DISTRIBUTION OF NATIONAL PRODUCT										
Distribution among A, M, and S										
10. Number of countries	7	6	6	8	8	10-11	12-13	13	14	30-32
Average Percentage Share of										
11. A sector	13.2	17.2	19.2	30.1	35.4	42.5	54.6	15.1	25.4	45.6
12. M sector	38.1	41.5	29.2	24.2	24.3	17.8	13.7	39.7	26.4	17.9
13. S sector	48.7	41.2	51.6	45.7	40.2	39.3	33.3	45.2	48.2	37.2

Table 5 (Cont'd)—Industrial Structure of Labor Force and of National Product; Countries Grouped by Product Per Capita (Based on Estimates in Current Prices, Averages for Post-World War II Years)

Sectors in Distribution of Labor Force and Income	Groups of Countries by Product Per Capita							Wider Groups		
	I (1)	II (2)	III (3)	IV (4)	V (5)	VI (6)	VII (7)	I+II (8)	III+IV (9)	V+VI+VII (10)
Distribution of S Sector										
14. Number of countries	4-6	5-6	5-6	8	4-6	8-9	10-12	9-11	13-14	22-27
Average Percentage Share of										
15. T division	9.5	9.9	8.4	6.7	8.2	4.4	3.3	9.7	7.4	4.4
16. C division	14.1	12.7	14.3	16.7	13.5	12.1	14.4	13.3	15.7	13.3
17. T+C division	23.6	22.3	21.6	23.4	21.4	15.9	17.6	22.8	22.6	17.7
18. OS division	26.6	18.9	30.0	22.3	20.4	23.4	15.7	22.0	25.6	19.3
III PRODUCT PER MEMBER OF LABOR FORCE, RELATIVE TO COUNTRYWIDE										
A Compared with M+S										
19. Number of countries	5	5	5	3	4	7	4	10	8	15
20. Average relative for A	0.92	0.85	0.75	0.59	0.75	0.79	1.00	0.89	0.69	0.84
21. Average relative for M+S	1.01	1.05	1.10	1.44	1.31	1.33	1.34	1.03	1.23	1.32
22. Average A/M+S ratio	0.95	0.81	0.70	0.45	0.61	0.65	0.89	0.88	0.60	0.70
M Compared with S										
23. Number of countries	5	5	5	3	4	7	3	10	8	14
24. Average relative for M	1.02	1.11	0.95	1.24	1.18	0.97	1.18	1.06	1.06	1.08
25. Average relative for S	1.02	0.98	1.19	1.54	1.39	1.60	1.52	1.00	1.32	1.52
26. Average M/S ratio	1.03	1.14	0.84	0.83	0.87	0.63	0.89	1.09	0.84	0.76
T+C Compared with OS										
27. Number of countries	3	5	5	3	3	6	3	8	8	12

28. Average relative for T+C	0.97	1.11	1.23	2.04	1.83	1.90	1.82	1.06	1.53	1.86
29. Average relative for OS	1.26	0.85	1.17	1.16	1.25	1.52	1.39	1.00	1.17	1.42
30. Average T+C/OS ratio	0.81	1.32	1.09	1.78	1.52	1.30	1.64	1.13	1.35	1.44
31. Measure of intersectoral inequality of income per member of labor force (based on A, M, T+C, and OS distribution)	17.9	13.9	22.3	43.2	28.2	30.5	27.8	16.1	31.6	29.2

The data are from Simon Kuznets, "Quantitative Aspects of the Economic Growth of Nations: II. Industrial Distribution of National Product and Labor Force," *Economic Development and Cultural Change*, Suppl. to Vol. V, No. 4 (July, 1957). This source should be consulted for more detailed data and explanation.

The grouping of countries by per capita product is based largely on United Nations sources: see United Nations, *Statistical Papers*, Series E, No. 4, 1957, for fifty-five countries and their per capita product in 1952-54; and *Statistical Papers*, Series E, No. 1, 1950, for seventy countries and their per capita product in 1949. A rough index of per capita product for the seven classes, with 100 for class VII, is: I—1,700; II—1,000; III—650; IV—400; V—270; VI—200; VII—100.

The A sector includes agriculture and related industries (fishing and forestry); the M sector includes mining, manufacturing, and construction; the S sector includes all the service activities. The subdivisions distinguished within the S sector are: T—transportation and communication; C—commerce, including wholesale and retail trade, banking, and finance; OS—other service activities (professional, personal, business, government).

The product totals are in most cases national income or net domestic product. The labor force excludes all unpaid family labor.

The percentage shares in national product and in labor force were calculated for each country separately; then arithmetic means (unweighted) of the shares were computed for each of the groups in columns 1-10.

The relative income per worker in a given sector or subdivision (relative to countrywide income per worker) is obtained by dividing the share of the sector in national product by its share in labor force. Such relatives were calculated for each sector and each country separately; the unweighted arithmetic means of these relatives are given in Panel III.

The measure of inequality in line 31 is obtained by subtracting the share of each sector in labor force from its share in national product, and then adding the differences regardless of signs. If one sector with only one worker gets all the income and the other sectors get none, the measure will be 200 minus (1/total number in labor force). If there is no intersectoral inequality, the index will be zero. The index was computed for each country separately, and the unweighted arithmetic means of such indexes are given in line 31.

Some of the findings in Tables 5-7 are by now quite familiar to economists, even those with only general knowledge of growth experience; others are perhaps less widely known. We first summarize the findings *seriatim;* and then discuss briefly some of the more interesting implications and problems suggested by them.

a) As we move from groups of countries with high per capita income to those with low, the share of the A sector in the labor force increases, while the shares of the M and the S sectors decrease. And the positive association between per capita product and the share of the S sector characterizes each subdivision distinguished in Table 5. In other words, in the more developed countries, the share of the A sector in labor force is low, and those of the M and S sectors are high; whereas the opposite is true of the less developed countries.

b) The *range* of differences in the shares of the several sectors should be noted. The widest range is in the share of the A sector: from less than 15 per cent in group I to over 60 per cent in group VII, i.e., more than 1 to 4. That in the share of the M sector is narrower—from over 40 to about 15 per cent, or less than 1 to 3. The narrowest range is in the share of the S sector—from 45 to about 24 per cent, or less than 1 to 2. Within the S sector, it is the OS division that is responsible for the narrow range of differences, and its share also shows the least regular association with per capita income. These differences are variations in responsiveness of the shares of various sectors in the labor force to per capita income. Thus they possibly reflect the response of these shares to the rise in per capita income in the process of modern economic growth.

c) The share of the A sector in national product is also

negatively correlated with income per capita, being low in countries with high per capita income and high in countries with low per capita income. Also, as in the labor force, the shares of the M and S sectors in national product are positively associated with income per capita, being high in groups I and II and low in groups VI and VII. Again, the relative range of differences from group I to group VII is widest in the share of the A sector and narrowest in the share of the S sector. The interesting and distinctive feature of the industrial structure of national income, in contrast with that of labor force, is in the behavior of the shares of the C and OS divisions of the S sector. There is *no* clear association between the share of the former in national product and per capita income: it varies around 14 per cent without any significant pattern. There is *some* positive association between per capita income and the share of the OS division in national product, but the range of differences in the share is quite narrow and the association does not appear to be truly systematic and significant. Thus, unlike the shares of the C and OS divisions in the labor force, which show distinct positive association with per capita income, their shares in national product are about the same in high and in low income countries, in the developed and in the underdeveloped. The positive association between the share of the *total* S sector in national product and per capita income is, therefore, chiefly accounted for by the movement of the share of the T division whose pattern of association with per capita income is very much like that of the share of the M sector.

d) By dividing the volume of product originating in a given sector by the number of workers (members of the

Table 6—Long-Term Changes in Shares of Major Sectors in Labor Force and in National Product; Selected Countries

COUNTRY	SHARES IN LABOR FORCE				SHARES IN NATIONAL PRODUCT			
	Date (1)	A (2)	M (3)	S (4)	Date (5)	A (6)	M (7)	S (8)
United Kingdom								
1. Initial period	1911	12	43	45	1895	10	37	53
2. Terminal period	1951	5	47	48	1948-54	6	46	48
3. Change		−7	+4	+3		−4	+9	−5
France								
4. Initial period	1866	52	29	20	1835	51	25	25
5. Terminal period	1950	33	34	33	1949	23	46	31
6. Change		−19	+5	+13		−28	+21	+6
Germany[a]								
7. Initial period	1882	42	36	22	1860-69	32	24	44
8. Terminal period	1933	29	41	30	1905-14	18	39	43
9. Change		−13	+5	+8		−14	+15	−1
Netherlands								
10. Initial period	1909	28	35	37	1913	16	27	57
11. Terminal period	1947	19	33	48	1947-54	13	41	46
12. Change		−9	−2	+11		−3	+14	−11
Denmark								
13. Initial period	1870-79	51	{ 49		1870-79	45	{ 55	
14. Terminal period	1947-52	40	60 }		1947-52	19	81 }	
15. Change		−11	+11			−26	+26	

Norway								
16. Initial period	1875	59	19	22	1910	24	25	51
17. Terminal period	1950	29	35	36	1950	14	37	49
18. Change		−30	+16	+14		−10	+12	−2
Sweden								
19. Initial period	1910	46	26	28	1869-71	43	16	41
20. Terminal period	1950	20	41	39	1949-51	13	50	37
21. Change		−26	+15	+11		−30	+34	−4
Italy								
22. Initial period	1871	62	24	14	1876-80	55	20	25
23. Terminal period	1954	41	31	28	1950-54	26	39	35
24. Change		−21	+7	+14		−29	+19	+10
Hungary								
25. Initial period	1900	59	17	24	1899-1901	49	23	28
26. Terminal period	1941	50	23	27	1939/40-1942/43	27	38	35
27. Change		−9	+6	+3		−22	+15	+7
United States								
28. Initial period	1870	50	25	25	1869 & 1879	20	21	59
29. Terminal period	1950	12	35	53	1947-54	7	38	55
30. Change		−38	+10	+28		−13	+17	−4
Canada								
31. Initial period	1871	50	13	37	1870	45	24	32
32. Terminal period	1950-53	21	35	44	1948-54	13	39	48
33. Change		−29	+22	+7		−32	+15	+16

Table 6 (Cont'd)—Long-Term Changes in Shares of Major Sectors in Labor Force and in National Product; Selected Countries

	COUNTRY	SHARES IN LABOR FORCE				SHARES IN NATIONAL PRODUCT			
		Date (1)	A (2)	M (3)	S (4)	Date (5)	A (6)	M (7)	S (8)
	Union of South Africa								
34.	Initial period	1911	59	16	25	1911/12	16	34	50
35.	Terminal period	1946	47	20	33	1944/45	12	34	54
36.	Change		—12	+4	+8		—4	0	+4
	Japan[b]								
37.	Initial period	1877 & 1882	83	6	11	1878-82	65	11	25
38.	Terminal period	1950	48	21	30	1947-54	24	32	44
39.	Change		—35	+15	+19		—41	+21	+19
	Australia								
40.	Initial period	1871	37	33	30	1891	37	18	45
41.	Terminal period	1933	22	35	43	1939	17	22	61
42.	Change		—15	+2	+13		—20	+4	+16
	New Zealand								
43.	Initial period	1874	31	41	28	1901	47	18	35
44.	Terminal period	1936	25	29	46	1936	35	12	53
45.	Change		—6	—12	+18		—12	—6	+18

For the basic source and definitions of sectors see the notes to Table 5.

Since the records for long periods are available largely for labor force including unpaid family labor, these totals were used in the present table. However, Colin Clark's data, available for labor force excluding women in agriculture, yield similar results.

a. Versailles territory for labor force; pre-World War I territory for national product.

b. Of the two sets of estimates for Japan (by Yamada and by Ohkawa), the one by Ohkawa was used since it was compiled more recently.

Table 7—Long-Term Changes in Sectoral Ratios of Income Per Worker and in Intersectoral Income Inequality; Selected Countries

COUNTRY	INTERVAL (approx.) (1)	A/M + S RATIO Initial (2)	A/M + S RATIO Terminal (3)	A/M + S RATIO Change (4)	M/S RATIO Initial (5)	M/S RATIO Terminal (6)	M/S RATIO Change (7)	MEASURE OF INEQUALITY Terminal (8)	MEASURE OF INEQUALITY Initial (9)	MEASURE OF INEQUALITY Change (10)
1. United Kingdom	1893-1950	0.60	1.08	+0.48	0.40	0.96	+0.56	1.6	44.8	—43.2
2. France	1895-1950	0.62	0.62	0	0.93	1.40	+0.47	24.0	24.0	0
3. Germany	1895-1935	0.36	0.40	+0.04	0.32	0.78	+0.46	30.6	60.0	—29.4
4. Netherlands	1910-1949	0.49	0.61	+0.12	0.48	1.26	+0.78	17.0	41.0	—24.0
5. Denmark	1895-1950	0.55	0.79	+0.24	n.a.	n.a.	n.a.	7.8	28.4	—20.6
6. Norway	1910-1950	0.35	0.39	+0.04	0.54	0.78	+0.24	31.6	46.0	—14.4
7. Sweden	1900-1950	0.34	0.59	+0.25	0.50	1.29	+0.79	17.8	51.8	—34.0
8. Italy	1900-1952	0.57	0.51	—0.06	0.49	1.05	+0.56	28.2	30.0	—1.8
9. Hungary	1900-1940	0.65	0.37	—0.28	1.15	1.23	+0.08	45.8	20.0	+25.8
10. United States	1900-1950	0.35	0.56	+0.21	0.50	1.05	+0.55	10.8	48.6	—37.8
11. Canada	1900-1950	0.67	0.61	—0.06	0.70	1.09	+0.39	14.0	22.0	—8.0
12. Union of South Africa	1911-1945	0.13	0.15	+0.02	1.15	1.03	—0.12	70.6	85.8	—15.2
13. Japan	1900-1950	0.40	0.34	—0.06	0.87	1.01	+0.14	48.0	43.0	+5.0
14. Australia	1891-1939	1.62	0.78	—0.84	0.84	0.93	+0.09	7.4	20.6	—13.2
15. New Zealand	1901-1936	2.13	1.60	—0.53	1.58	0.83	—0.75	20.0	36.8	—16.8

For the basic source and definitions of sectors see the notes to Table 5.

The period covered is indicated only approximately in column 1. The data for shares in labor force and in income at the beginning and end of the period are sometimes given for slightly different dates. For more detail see the source noted in Table 5, particularly Table 22.

The measures of inequality shown in columns 8-10 are based on the distinction among the three major sectors alone (A, M, and S).

labor force) attached to it, we secure, of course, product per worker for the sector. By dividing the percentage share of a given sector in national product by its percentage share in the labor force, we secure the *ratio* of product per worker in the sector to product per worker for the country as a whole. Lines 20-22 of Table 5 show that relative product per worker in the A sector is below 1.0 in most countries, i.e., lower than countrywide product per worker; and that in all groups it is lower than product per worker in the non-agricultural sectors combined. What is even more interesting, the relative disparity in product per worker between the A sector and the non-agricultural sectors tends to be wider in the low income than in the high income countries. An important consequence follows: wide as the disparities are in total income per worker between developed and underdeveloped countries, the disparities between them in product per worker in the A sector are even wider, while those in product per worker in the M + S sector are narrower. To put it differently, the underdeveloped countries are further behind the developed countries in product per worker in agriculture than they are in product per worker in the non-agricultural sectors.

e) In comparing product per worker in the M and S sectors, we find that the latter is usually higher than the former (lines 24-26). Furthermore, the difference between the S and M sectors in product per worker is narrowest in the high income, developed countries, and widest in the low income, underdeveloped countries. Searching for the more specific locus of this difference, we find that the T + C division of the S sector is characterized by generally higher levels of product per worker than the OS division (lines

28-30), and here again the relative excess is inversely related to income per capita—being lowest in the high income, developed countries and highest in the low income, underdeveloped countries.

f) If income per worker were the same in all sectors within a country, the percentage distributions of the country's labor force and national product would be identical; if we subtracted the share in product for each sector from its share in labor force, the difference would be zero. If incomes per worker in the several sectors of the country's economy are unequal, a weighted measure of inequality (weighted by the share of each sector in the labor force) is derived as the sum of differences, signs disregarded, between the share of each sector in labor force and in national product respectively. We calculated such a measure of intersectoral inequality of income per worker for each country (distinguishing the A sector, the M sector, and the T+C and OS subdivisions of the S sector), and then averaged these measures for groups I-VII (line 31). Clearly, intersectoral inequality in income per worker is narrowest in the high income, developed countries and rather wide in the low income, underdeveloped countries.

The sample of long-term records, from which the changes in the industrial structure of labor force and national product summarized in Tables 6 and 7 were derived, suffers from at least five defects. First, only fifteen countries are included. Second, even among these, at least two—Australia and New Zealand—are atypical with respect to their industrial structure, as is evidenced by the extremely high relative level of per worker product in the A sector in the earlier decades (see lines 14 and 15, column 2 of Table 7). Third, the periods for many countries are too short in that they do not cover the earlier phases of the shift away from agriculture. Fourth, the estimates for some countries are subject to wide margins of error in the earlier decades. Fifth, the records do not permit us to distinguish subdivisions within the S sector. Nevertheless, it is possible to draw a rough outline of the secular pattern of change in industrial structure accompanying economic growth.

g) In all fifteen countries, without exception, the shares of the A sector in both labor force and national product declined. In most countries (with one or two exceptions) the shares of the M sector in labor force and national product rose. However, the rise in the share of the M sector in the labor force was not as large as might have been expected from the cross-section analysis in Table 5. Finally, the share of the S sector in the labor force rose in all countries, but its share in national product showed no such consistent movement. Of the fourteen countries in which the share in national product can be distinguished, it rose in eight but declined in six; among the latter are some of the most advanced countries of the world—the United Kingdom, Germany, Netherlands, Sweden, and the United States. Thus, the limited association in cross-section analysis between per capita income and the share of the S sector in national product, observed in Table 5, is here translated to a rather diverse movement of the share over time in different countries. It follows that while economic growth is generally associated with a decline in the share of the A sector both in labor force and income, with a rise in the share of the M sector, more conspicuous in income than in the labor force, and with a rise in the share of the S sector in the labor force, it is not necessarily accompanied by a rise in the share of the S sector in national product.

h) If we exclude the exceptional cases of Australia and New Zealand, we find in most countries a *rise* in income per worker in the A sector, relative to that in the non-agricultural sectors (in eight of the thirteen countries with no change in another in Table 7, columns 2-4). This means that large as the rise in per worker product has been in the non-agricultural sectors, the rise in per worker product in the A sector has been even greater. Furthermore, within the non-agricultural part of the economy, the rise in the per worker product in the M sector was greater than that in the per worker product in the S sector, in all but two of the fourteen countries for which the comparison can be made. Thus the rise in per worker product in the S sector was more moderate than that in either the M or the A sector.

i) The trends in relative income per worker in the A, M, and S sectors just listed are opposite, as it were, to the *relative levels* indicated in Table 5: it is the level of income per worker in the A sector that is relatively the lowest; that in the S sector, the highest. This inverse relationship between differences in trends and differences in levels means, of course, *convergence* over time, i.e., reduction in intersectoral inequality in income per worker. And the latter is clearly indicated in columns 8-10 of Table 7: in all but three of the fifteen countries, our measure of inequality declines, and in one of the three exceptions no change is shown. Thus, in respect to the movements of sectoral levels of income per worker, the trends shown by the long-term records are consistent with what we would expect from the cross-section analysis in Table 5.

SOME QUESTIONS
AND IMPLICATIONS

Of the several questions and implications suggested by the findings summarized above (and the more detailed evidence available elsewhere), three may be selected for brief discussion. The first is the well-known shift away from agriculture, associated with rise in income per capita during the course of economic growth which led to the identification of the latter with "industrialization," "urbanization," and associated processes. Without dealing thoroughly with the wide complex of trends involved and factors underlying them, one may well ask what *major* forces were at play. The second is the less familiar finding relating to the narrow range of differences in the shares of the S sector in labor force and national income, in response to differences in per capita income; and the corresponding diversity of trends over time in the share of the S sector in national income. The third is the reasons for, and implications of, the much wider intersectoral inequality in per worker product in underdeveloped than in developed countries, and hence for the reduction in such inequality that usually accompanies economic growth.

a) If real income per worker and hence per capita increases, the demand for products of sectors other than agriculture is likely to rise more than the demand for the products of agriculture. Hence, in a *closed* economy, a rise in per capita real income will be accompanied by shifts in the structure of total output from the A sector; even in an *open* economy the advantages of location mean that the shift of total demand will favor a greater share of domestic output for the non-agricultural sectors. If the demand shifts away from the A sector, the share of the latter in real income will decline, and so will its share in the labor force unless productivity per unit of labor falls—which is unlikely. This is the customary explanation of the decline in the share of the A sector in labor force and national income as an application of the Engel law to processes of income change over time (rather than to differences in cross-section analysis).

There is, however, another link to this argument that is perhaps not always kept in mind; it has to do with the condition for the rise in product per worker, and hence in per capita product. In a closed economy with a large proportion of the labor force in the A sector, i.e., in an underdeveloped or pre-industrial economy with, say, 80 per cent of all workers in agriculture, the implication is that 80 workers feed 100 workers and their families. Under such conditions, a rise in total product per worker must be limited unless it reflects a rise in product per worker in the A sector. It is a pre-condition of industrialization as a world-wide phenomenon that productivity of labor in *agriculture* increases sufficiently to feed, at higher per capita levels, a larger proportion of the labor force than could be fed before. And as our estimates have shown, in most of the developed countries, product per worker in the A sector increased *more* than product per worker in the rest of the economy combined. At the danger of stressing the obvious, one may claim that an agricultural revolution —a marked rise in productivity per worker in agriculture— is a pre-condition of the industrial revolution for any sizable region in the world; surely so for any country in which (as is the case with many underdeveloped or less developed countries today) the product per worker in the A sector is so distressingly low as to tie to the land, at low income levels, a large part of the population and leave little margin for the non-agricultural sector to grow upon. Conversely, when modern economic growth does occur, it is the combination of the marked rise in productivity of labor in the A sector, with the secular limits on the demand for its products that results in such a sharp and uniform reduction of the A sector in the labor force.

There would be no need to stress this obvious point if countries concerned with furthering economic growth were not concentrating on building up large-scale manufacturing plants and similar conspicuous items of an industrial economy. Such preoccupation with the non-agricultural sectors of the economy may easily and rapidly lead to an imbalance between a few advanced production sectors and underdeveloped agriculture. This imbalance manifests itself in inflationary trends in prices of food and other agricultural products whose supply remains inelastic, in narrow markets for the industrial goods, and in a continuance of population pressure on land. While it is true that increased productivity on land and the resulting surplus population to be drained off the farms necessitate employment opportunities elsewhere, this problem is scarcely resolved by efforts concentrated on, or largely limited to, the setting up of a small number of advanced industrial plants usually characterized by high capital and low labor intensity.

b) Several reasons may be adduced to explain the narrow range of differences in the share of the S sector associated with differences in per capita income. First, the products of the S sector are less easily imported and exported than are the commodity products of the A and M sectors. To be sure, some services are embodied in values of commodities, and can thus also be exported or imported. But many others—government, professional, personal, retail distribution, and similar services—cannot move across a country's boundaries. The international division of labor thus permits a country to concentrate on either the A or the M sector, but not to dispense with a sizable minimum of S sector goods that must be produced at home. Second, the S sector includes a wide variety of miscellaneous activities, some of which may be in larger supply in low income countries than in high, e.g., domestic and personal services, religious services, and the like; and others of which may be in large supply in high income countries, e.g., the professional, educational, and business services. A third and related factor bears particularly upon the share in the labor force. The pressure of population on land and the surplus labor force in the less developed countries may mean a movement into service activities since some of them demand little capital and yet provide some modicum of living (peddling, cart transport, personal services of various descriptions), and since the employment of this surplus in the M sector is inhibited partly by capital scarcity and partly by competition of the M sector in the more developed countries. A fourth factor is of particular bearing upon the share of the S sector in national income. Despite the inclusion of large groups of low-paid activities, the average income per worker in the S sector in the underdeveloped countries is higher, relative to the per worker income in other sectors, than in the developed countries. This is due to the extremely high relative income of some groups within the S sector of the underdeveloped countries. (The reasons for these high relative incomes will be discussed below.)

Given the heterogeneity of the S sector, and the difficulty in moving its goods across a country's boundaries, it may be that economic growth is not necessarily accompanied through all phases by a rise in the share of the S sector in either labor force or national income. In that sense our finding of diversity of movement of the share in national income requires no further explanation. It is, rather, the finding that the share in the labor force tends to rise fairly generally that requires further discussion. Why should the growth of an economy be accompanied by such a consistent shift of labor into service activities?

The explanation lies in the increase of productivity in the A and M sectors. In general, this increase is attained, particularly in the M sector, by concentration of production in large-scale units, with elaborate capital equipment, and by a continuity of the mass-scale operation indispensable for low cost per product unit and hence for high output per labor input. Such concentration in scale and continuity in time require a large volume of ancillary services—transportation, communication, distribution, etc.—that bridge the time and space gaps between (1) seasonally and otherwise affected supplies of agricultural materials and their use in the production processes, and (2) seasonally and otherwise affected demand for final products and their continuous flow out of the productive system. Furthermore, increasing urbanization calls for increased government services; the demand for an educated population and labor force increases service activities in education; the generally greater complexity of the economic system requires more supervision by government in the way of legislation, regulation, and administration. Thus, over and above any shift in demand by ultimate consumers in favor of services that may occur with a rise in real income per capita, there is perhaps the more important rise in the demand for service activities as a necessary complement to the concentrated and specialized high-level productivity organization in the A and M sectors. Given greater demand for the products of the S sector, and a somewhat lesser increase in per worker productivity in many divisions of this sector than in the A and M sectors, the shift in the labor force toward higher proportions in the S sector is easily explained.

An intriguing corollary of this point should be noted. In the developed countries, a rise in the share of the S sector in the labor force may be viewed as due largely to demands originating *because* of a shift toward more highly productive organization in the A and M sectors and is, in a sense, necessary for the latter. In other words, the shift of the labor force toward the S sector is an indispensable concomitant of the movement toward higher productivity levels throughout the economy. In the less developed countries, there may be long periods of rise in the share of the S sector in the labor force, not because it is a necessary complement to increasingly higher levels of technology and productivity in the A and M sectors, but only because population pressure on land and the limitations of employment opportunities in the M sector drive the surplus labor into low-paid service activities. To be sure, such a shift from enforced idleness on the land to some activity, however minor, in the cities may still constitute a net gain in national productivity. And yet, there is a world of difference between a rise in the share of the S sector produced by surplus population pressures and a rise called for by the demands of high-level technology in agriculture and manufacturing.

c) In the lower income, underdeveloped countries, despite the fact that the S sector includes larger proportions than elsewhere of extremely low-paid occupations, the product per worker for the sector as a whole is appreciably higher than in the other parts of the economy. This means necessarily that in some divisions of the S sector product per worker (including entrepreneurs) must be extremely high relative to the countrywide product per worker. This is true in the commerce division (trade, banking, etc.) and in the professional and government subdivisions.

There are two major reasons why product per worker in these selected divisions of the S sector is so much higher relative to the countrywide average in the less than in the more developed countries. First, the commerce division in the less developed countries may be dominated by traders, landlords, and money lenders who constitute a group of entrepreneurs. Under conditions of capital scarcity and the economically weak position of the large masses of agricultural cultivators, small handicraftsmen, and shopkeepers, these entrepreneurs enjoy a monopoly position and a great economic advantage that may secure for them returns that, while absolutely smaller per head than those in the developed countries, nevertheless are a much larger multiple of the per worker income for the country as a whole. No such monopoly advantages and superior economic power attach to similar groups in the better-organized, advanced economies of the developed countries. Second, among certain occupations in the S sector, particularly the professional, minimum levels of income are required for the adequate pursuit of activity, and these minimum levels are a larger multiple of the countrywide income per capita or per worker in the less developed than in the more developed countries. Thus a university professor in India, with an annual salary of say seven to eight thousand rupees is receiving an income that is in absolute terms much lower than the seven to eight thousand dollars received by a university professor in the United States. But since per worker income in India is not much more than one thousand rupees, the Indian professor's salary is from seven to eight times the countrywide average; whereas with per worker income in the United States close to five thousand dollars, the professor's salary in that country is less than twice the countrywide average. Since the S sector of the less developed countries includes large groups whose occupation requires substantial minimum levels of absolute income per capita, the very low level of the countrywide income per capita or per worker means that these groups are quite high in the array by relative income position within the country. Furthermore, the connection between the scarcity advantages of occupations requiring a substantial capital investment in education and training and the high levels of their relative income position is much closer in the underdeveloped than in the developed countries.

It follows that in the process of economic growth the increasing supply of capital, both for material investment and for investment in human beings, means a substantial reduction in the factors just adduced to explain why certain groups within the S sector in the underdeveloped countries secure per worker incomes so much higher than the countrywide average. The increased employment opportunities for large groups of the population, at places in the economy where they can be provided with substantial capital per head, mean a greater rise in the per worker product in both the A and M sectors than in the S sector.

The wide intersectoral inequality in product per worker in the less developed countries suggests that general inequality in the distribution of income by size in these countries may also be quite wide, perhaps wider than in the developed countries. This would be particularly true of recent periods, and in terms of income after taxes (disposable income) since taxes in the developed, high income countries, are generally far more progressive than in the less developed areas. Even if the purely statistical measures of relative income inequality showed inequality in the low income, underdeveloped countries *no wider* than in the high income, developed nations, the welfare implications would still be much more serious for the underdeveloped areas. If the countrywide real income per capita is low, the effects of inequality on the welfare position of the masses of the population whose income is significantly below the average are far more serious in terms of material deprivation than in countries where the average income is higher. To be sure, one cannot pass simply and directly from measures of product per worker originating in the various sectors to differences in income received by various groups within the population: income originating includes returns on assets which do not necessarily accrue to the members of the labor force attached to a given sector. But in all countries compensation of employees and entrepreneurial incomes account for by far the largest proportion of total income originating (or of net product turned out), the ratios usually being about 80 per cent. The proportions of total product that are not distributed (retained as corporate savings or government profits) or are distributed to the small group of pure *rentiers* usually do not amount to more than a few percentage points of national product. Therefore, the intersectoral inequality in product per worker shown in Tables 5 and 7, and discussed above, is highly suggestive of inequality in the distribution of income by size among the individuals and households who comprise a country's population. If this is true, the earlier inference that inequality in the size distribution of income is possibly wider in the underdeveloped than in the developed areas, and the conclusion that such inequality is reduced in the course of economic growth (as suggested by the narrowing of intersectoral inequality in product per worker shown by the trends in Table 7), are both plausible.

Lecture IV

CAPITAL FORMATION
PROPORTIONS—A
CROSS-SECTION VIEW

CAPITAL FOR any given country, as commonly measured, includes: (1) all construction and improvements attached to the land (buildings, dams, roads, fences, improvement of the soil, etc.); (2) machinery and equipment in the hands of producers, private and public, within the country, but not durable goods in the hands of households; (3) inventories within the country in the hands of business enterprises and governments, although for lack of data government inventories are frequently omitted; (4) net balance of claims against foreign countries. The sum of (1) and (2) is domestic fixed capital; the sum of (1), (2), and (3) is total domestic capital; the sum of (1), (2), (3), and (4) is total national capital. Capital formation designates additions to the stock of capital so defined, *gross* if current consumption of fixed capital is not deducted, *net* if such a deduction is made. Additions to inventories and to claims against foreign countries are always taken net. We can thus have gross or net domestic capital formation—a sum of gross or net additions to (1) and (2) with the net additions to (3), and gross or net national capital formation, a sum of gross or net additions to (1) and (2) with the net additions to (3) and (4).

Capital formation is measured by the flow of resources into it. Gross and net domestic capital formation are properly parts of gross and net domestic product, differing from national product in that they exclude the flow of factor shares across the nation's boundaries. Gross and net capital formation (national) are components of gross and net national product and represent the part of the latter that is saved, i.e., retained for use in further production. The remaining components of national product are flow of goods to ultimate consumers (individuals and households) and, in the most generally used definition, consumption by government—the two together forming the part of current product that is consumed rather than saved.

In the study of economic growth, wide interest attaches to the proportion that capital formation constitutes of national product. The larger it is (i.e., the larger the part of current product retained for use in further production), other conditions being equal, the higher the rate of growth of national product that can be generated. Low capital formation proportions mean low rates of growth of national product, unless capital-output ratios decline, i.e., unless more output can be turned out per unit of capital.

Table 8 summarizes evidence on capital formation proportions for the countries covered by post-World War II estimates. It is based on the usual procedure of calculating for each country the ratio of capital formation (or any other associated numerator) to the relevant national product total (or some corresponding denominator), and then computing arithmetic means (unweighted) of these ratios for countries grouped by per capita income. In summarizing the findings here, we emphasize the results for countries excluding colonies and certain units (e.g., Israel) whose exceptional experience may distort the average.

a) The ratio of gross domestic capital formation to gross domestic product is positively associated with income per capita, being higher for the high income, developed countries than for the low income, underdeveloped countries. It ranges from over 20 per cent in groups I and II to less than 12 per cent in group VII. The wider grouping shows a decline from over 22 per cent for groups I and II to less than 16 per cent for groups V, VI, and VII.

b) The ratio of net changes in claims against foreign countries to gross domestic product shows no definite association with income per capita. However, the share is quite minor and differences among the groups of countries are small.

c) The proportion of gross national capital formation to gross national product, i.e., the gross savings ratio, is positively associated with income per capita. The range is from over 20 per cent for groups I and II to about 12 per cent for group VII. For the wider grouping, the range is between close to 22 per cent for groups I and II and about 15 per cent for groups V, VI, and VII.

d) The estimate of current consumption of fixed capital is subject to wider error and more arbitrary assumptions than any other estimate in Table 8. This may be the reason for the somewhat erratic behavior of the proportion of net capital formation to net national product. In any case, it ranges from over 15 per cent in groups I and II to about 11 per cent in groups V, VI, and VII (and 7 per cent in group VII).

Table 8—*Average Ratios of Capital Formation to Domestic or National Product; Countries Grouped by Product Per Capita (Based on Estimates in Current Prices, Averages for Post-World War II Years, Mostly 1950-55)*

| RATIO | GROUPS OF COUNTRIES BY PRODUCT PER CAPITA | | | | | | | WIDER GROUPS | | |
	I (1)	II (2)	III (3)	IV (4)	V (5)	VI (6)	VII (7)	I+II (8)	III+IV (9)	V+VI+VII (10)
A. ALL COUNTRIES										
I Gross Capital Formation										
1. Number of countries	8	7	6	9	4	7	5	15	15	16
2. Average ratio, G.D.C.F./G.D.P. (per cent)	21.3	23.3	17.2	15.7	18.2	17.1	13.3	22.2	16.3	16.2
3. Average ratio, net change in foreign claims to G.D.C.F. (per cent)	0.8	−5.3	−40.4	−1.1	−18.4	−1.7	−29.7	−2.1	−16.9	−14.6
4. Average ratio, net change in foreign claims to G.D.P. (per cent)	0.0	−1.3	−7.4	−1.1	−2.2	−1.5	−2.1	−0.6	−3.6	−1.8
5. Average ratio, G.N.C.F./G.N.P. (per cent)	21.3	22.2	9.8	14.8	16.0	16.3	11.6	21.7	12.8	14.8
II Net Capital Formation										
6. Number of countries	6	5	5	5	2	5	4	11	10	11
7. Average ratio, cap. cons./G.D.F.C.F. (per cent)	43.4	32.3	38.4	34.4	36.4	38.5	46.2	38.4	36.4	40.9
8. Average ratio, N.N.C.F./G.N.C.F (per cent)	62.1	64.2	−2.3	60.4	36.2	61.7	38.1	63.1	29.1	48.5
9. Average ratio, N.N.C.F./N.N.P. (per cent)	14.5	16.0	3.1	8.9	11.5	11.9	12.3	15.2	6.0	12.0
B. COUNTRIES EXCLUDING COLONIES AND EXCEPTIONAL CASES										
I Gross Capital Formation										
10. Number of countries	8	7	4	9	3	5	2	15	13	10

11.	Average ratio, G.D.C.F./ G.D.P. (per cent)	21.3	23.3	16.2	15.7	20.0	14.4	11.4	22.2	15.9	15.5
12.	Average ratio, net change in foreign claims to G.D.C.F. (per cent)	0.6	−5.3	−17.7	−1.1	−3.0	−5.9	−15.6	−2.2	−6.2	−7.0
13.	Average ratio, net change in foreign claims to G.D.P. (per cent)	0.0	−1.3	−2.8	−1.1	−0.2	−0.9	0.4	−0.6	−1.6	−0.4
14.	Average ratio, G.N.C.F./ G.N.P. (per cent)	21.3	22.2	13.3	14.8	19.8	13.9	11.8	21.7	14.3	15.2
	II Net Capital Formation										
15.	Number of countries	6	5	3	5	1	4	2	11	8	7
16.	Average ratio, cap. cons./ G.D.F.C.F. (per cent)	43.4	32.3	46.9	34.4	33.1	44.0	65.3	38.4	39.1	48.5
17.	Average ratio, N.N.C.F./ G.N.C.F. (per cent)	62.1	64.2	44.9	60.4	76.4	58.6	−4.6	63.1	54.6	43.1
18.	Average ratio, N.N.C.F./ N.N.P. (per cent)	14.5	16.0	6.1	8.9	23.2	9.7	7.0	15.2	7.9	10.9

The basic source is United Nations, "Statistics of National Income and Expenditure," *Statistical Papers, Series H*, No. 10 (January, 1957). Data for 46 countries were used, excluding those with less than one million population.

The various capital formation and product totals were added for the post-World War II years given (usually 1950-55) and the ratios of the period totals calculated. The proportions are, therefore, weighted by the magnitude of the denominator in each year. The countries were then grouped by their product per capita, and unweighted arithmetic means of the ratios were calculated for each group.

The capital formation totals employed in the table are: G.D.F.C.F.—gross domestic fixed capital formation; G.D.C.F.—gross domestic capital formation (including additions to inventories); G.N.C.F.—gross national capital formation, i.e., gross domestic plus net changes in claims against foreign countries; N.N.C.F.—net national capital formation (net of capital consumption). The various product totals used are: G.D.P.—gross domestic product (excluding net movement of factor incomes abroad); G.N.P.—gross national product; N.N.P.—net national product. All the totals are in current market prices.

Panel B excludes colonies and some exceptional cases. Specifically, the countries excluded are: Puerto Rico and Israel (group III); Jamaica (group V); Rhodesia and Nyasaland, and the Gold Coast (group VI); Nigeria, South Korea, and the Belgian Congo (group VII).

As it stands, the evidence in Table 8 accords with our expectations, and with the emphasis, in much recent literature on economic growth, placed on the importance of raising the capital formation proportions in the less developed countries. Yet the results, if interpreted as suggestive of differences in the *long-term* levels of capital formation proportions, are puzzling.

The differences in the capital formation proportions are quite small: the share of net capital formation in net national product in groups I and II exceeds that in group VII by 8 per cent of national product, and the range for the share of gross capital formation in gross national product is about 10 per cent of gross national product. Is it plausible to assume that these few additional percentage points account for the striking differences in levels of performance and patterns of growth that we observe between the developed and the underdeveloped economies? Of course, one could reply in terms of the old parable that for want of a horseshoe nail, a kingdom was lost; I must confess, however, to a strong intuitive objection to such a theory of history or of economic growth that puts its faith in the strategic importance of minor details.

If this reaction is discounted as too intuitive, consider a second, more "sophisticated" illustration that takes for granted the cardinal importance of capital accumulation. Assume that the range from 15 to 7.5 or even 5 per cent describes the *long-term* net capital formation proportions in the developed and in the underdeveloped countries. Assume also that the reproducible capital-output ratio is constant over time and the *same* in both sets of countries —an assumption unfavorable to the conclusions that the example is to illustrate. Then, according to the Harrod-

Domar formula, the "permitted" rate of growth of national product in the underdeveloped countries would be either one-half or one-third of the rate of growth of national product in the developed countries. If, however, the capital-output ratio is somewhat higher in the latter than in the former (say 3 to 1 compared with 2.5 to 1), the permitted rate of growth of national product would be either 2 or 3 per cent per year in the underdeveloped countries, compared with 5 per cent in the developed countries. The implicit difference in the rate of growth of product *per capita* would then depend upon the difference in the rate of growth of population. We know that in many major underdeveloped countries, e.g., India and China, the rate of growth of population over the last century was appreciably lower than that in many developed countries. A rate of population growth of 10 to 15 per cent per decade was not unusual for developed countries. If we assume that the corresponding rate for such countries as India and China was between 5 and 7.5 per cent per decade, the implicit rate of growth of *per capita* income for such underdeveloped countries would not be much lower than the high rates we observed for the developed countries. Even if we assume the same rate of population growth for the two groups of countries, the implicit rate of growth in per capita income for the underdeveloped areas still seems too high. We observed that rates of growth of per capita income of 15 to 20 per cent per decade in the developed areas were not uncommon. On the basis of 15 per cent, with a range for capital formation proportions of 2.5 to 1 (i.e., 15 to 6 per cent net, or 22 to 9 per cent gross), and identical rates of growth of total population, we derive a rate of growth in per capita income in the underdeveloped countries of 6 per cent per decade—which would cumulate over a century to a rise of almost 80 per cent. No such substantial rise in per capita product can have occurred in the underdeveloped countries (with more than half of the world's population) in which per capita income today is about $100 (in 1952-54 prices).

The preceding comments, although quite sketchy, suggest two inferences. The first is that the findings in Table 8, if taken as evidence of long-term levels and differences in capital formation proportions, may overstate these proportions for the underdeveloped countries and hence understate the range between them and the proportions in the developed countries. The second is that the measures as they stand are, by definition, inadequate gauges of capital conceived as a tool of economic growth. The first inference can be discussed only in terms of data on long-term levels of capital proportions in the low income countries, and no such data are at hand. The only observation that can be made is that the capital formation proportions for the less developed countries in Table 8, which relates to the prosperous 1950's, may be significantly higher than they were over the long periods in the past.

The second inference can be discussed and should shed some light on important aspects of current measurement and analysis of capital formation. One possible limitation of the measures may lie in their scope. In particular, it may be argued that residential housing is not in a class with industrial plants and other construction, machinery and equipment, and even inventories, as a tool for furthering economic growth. Furthermore, if too much capital formation goes into residential housing in the less developed countries, the range in the proportion of additions to *real* tools for further growth may be wider than that shown in Table 8. However, the available data do not support this hypothesis. For 22 countries in post-World War II years (from the source used for Table 8) the share of residential construction in domestic gross fixed capital formation averages about 21 per cent; for 12 countries in groups I and II, the average is 22 per cent; for 5 countries in groups III and IV (excluding Israel) the average is 26 per cent; and for 5 countries in groups V-VII, it is 16 per cent. The meagre evidence, as far as it goes, actually shows that residential construction is a smaller proportion of capital formation in the less developed countries. Nor are there decisive differences between the high and low income countries in the share of total construction as distinct from machinery and equipment: for the 27 countries for which we have data, the share in domestic gross fixed capital formation averages 59 per cent; for 10 countries in groups I and II—53 per cent; for 9 countries in groups III and IV—64 per cent; and for 8 countries in groups V, VI, and VII—60 per cent.

More significant than the possible sins of commission are the sins of omission—the limitations of the measures because they do not reflect other important factors in economic growth. We mention four major omissions—and there are certainly others. First, many uses of current product, besides those included in capital formation as defined above, contribute to economic growth by improving the quality and skill of the labor force and by increasing the efficiency of a complex productive system. At least part of the expenditures for education, research (by nonprofit institutions), health, recreation, and even some items of food, clothing, housing, and personal services (all now included in consumer outlay) belong here, as well as some government consumption when it is included in national product. With per capita product and consumption so much higher in the developed than in the underdeveloped countries, there is more room in the former for proportionately greater growth-furthering (rather than life-maintaining) types of expenditure among the outlays by ultimate consumers and governments. Since the share of total consumption in net national product ranges from 85 to well over 90 per cent, and that in gross national product from 78 to somewhat below 90 per cent, the wide differences that are possible in the capital-element shares of consumption may well overshadow the differences in capital formation proportions as measured in Table 8. Thus if a quarter of the consumption component in the developed countries were growth-furthering, the gross capital investment proportion (using the more inclusive concept of capital) would be raised from 22 to 42 per cent of gross national product; and, by analogy, the net capital investment proportion would be raised from 15 to 28 per cent of net national product. In the underdeveloped countries on the other hand, the generous allowance of a tenth of the consumption component as growth-furthering would raise the gross capital formation proportion from 11 to 20 per cent, and the net capital formation proportion (again by analogy) from 7 to 13 per cent. The *relative* discrepancy between the capital formation proportions in the two sets of countries is not affected much, but the *weight* of the difference in national product increases appreciably. However, the point to be stressed is that capital investment, viewed as a tool of economic growth, involves more than capital formation in the standard definition followed in

Table 8: it penetrates much more deeply into other uses of national product and into investment in human beings.

Second, as measured above, capital and capital formation do not include natural resources; they only include investments in developing the latter. In some underdeveloped countries, where the ratio of population to land may be high, additions to *reproducible capital* may not yield as high a rate of additions to final product as in countries where the limiting pressure of natural resources is not as great. In other underdeveloped countries, where natural resources may be relatively more abundant and there is no pressure of population on land, the rate of population growth may be higher (particularly in recent decades) than in the developed countries. Thus, in one case, the effect of the capital formation proportions on per capita income may be reduced by relative scarcity of natural resources, which in turn may affect even the rates of population growth; in the other case, it may be reduced by a high rate of population growth.

Third, we have assumed a constant capital-output ratio. But in some phases of economic growth this ratio may well rise because long-lived fixed investments in sectors like housing, roads, transport, communication, and some branches of manufacturing must be made on a large scale. For several decades the increasing weight of such sectors will tend to raise the countrywide capital-output ratio— particularly the marginal one. In simple terms, this means that given rises in national product will require more than proportional additions to capital stock and a higher capital formation proportion than before. In other phases, the capital-output ratio may decline because the basic framework of long-lived capital investment will have been completed, and economy in capital use may be increasingly introduced. In the United States, for example, the country-wide capital-output ratio rose from the 1880's to World War I and declined from the early 1920's to date. If the low income countries in Table 8 are in the phase in which heavy capital investments are the indispensable step forward, and a rising capital-output ratio is thus in order, adequate economic growth may require higher capital formation proportions than equal growth in the more developed countries.

Finally, if we view national capital formation proportions as national savings ratios, it should be emphasized that the underlying aggregates conceal potentially important differences among countries in the flow of money savings and in patterns of their utilization. Given the possibly wider inequality in the size distribution of income in the less developed countries, the proportions to national income of gross savings originating among the upper income groups may well be higher than (or at least equal to, or not much smaller than) those in the more developed countries. The crucial difference may be in the patterns of utilization of such savings. In the less developed countries a greater proportion of these savings may finance consumption needs of the lower income groups, in return for the shift of land and other assets into the hands of the money lenders; or a greater proportion of such savings may go into hoards of precious metals and ornaments rather than into productive investment. Moreover, with the inadequate development of organized banking and other financial intermediaries, and reliance upon personal ties rather than upon impersonal financial institutions, the channeling of savings available for investment may not be as productive, as conducive to growth, as that in the developed countries. The mobility of such savings may not be as high, and they may not flow as freely to those uses that are most promising in terms of the national product. Some evidence in support of this statement might be found if we had more detailed information on the flow of savings and the various channels and types of investment in a variety of countries, for the full range from the high income, developed groups to the low income, underdeveloped groups.

LONG-TERM TRENDS IN CAPITAL FORMATION PROPORTIONS

Many of the comments above apply also to the long-term trends of capital formation proportions. Clearly, capital formation, as usually measured, does not reflect the full range of uses of national product that contribute in the course of time to the economic growth of a country; there must be changing phases, accompanied by changes in the capital-output ratio; there must also be long-term trends in the interplay between savings and capital investment.

Nevertheless, long-term records of capital formation proportions for a number of countries do shed light on several questions that we raised but could not answer in the preceding section. Unfortunately our long-term records of capital formation are poor. Table 9 includes only eight countries, and even for some of these the periods are short and the coverage incomplete. Furthermore, the evidence reveals wide differences in the long-term trends. Even if we disregard the figures for 1950-55 as relating to too short a period, we find in some countries, e.g., Sweden, the United Kingdom, Italy, and Canada, that the proportion of gross capital formation to gross national product

Table 9—Long-Term Changes in Proportions of Capital Formation and Net Movements in Foreign Claims to Domestic or National Product; Selected Countries (Based on Totals in Current Prices)

COUNTRY AND PERIOD	G.D.C.F. G.N.P. (1)	NET CHANGE IN FOREIGN CLAIMS G.D.C.F. (2)	NET CHANGE IN FOREIGN CLAIMS G.N.P. (3)	G.N.C.F. G.N.P. (4)	NET CHANGE IN FOREIGN CLAIMS N.N.P. (5)	N.N.C.F. N.N.P. (6)
United Kingdom[a]						
1. 1870-99	9.8	30.5	2.9	12.8	3.0	11.0
2. 1890-1913	9.9	38.0	3.7	13.6	3.8	11.9
3. 1950-55	14.3	2.6	0.3	14.7	0.4	7.2
France						
4. 1853-78	n.a.	n.a.	n.a.	n.a.	1.4	9.9
5. 1878-1903	n.a.	n.a.	n.a.	n.a.	2.3	6.9
6. 1903-11	n.a.	n.a.	n.a.	n.a.	4.0	9.7
7. 1950-55	18.3	—4.7	—0.9	17.4	n.a.	n.a.
Denmark (net domestic product in col. 5 and 6)						
8. 1870-99	13.5	—13.6	—1.8	11.6	—1.9	7.5
9. 1900-29	12.9	—10.2	—1.3	11.6	—1.4	5.9
10. 1915-39	11.8	+0.7	+0.1	11.9	+0.1	6.3
11. 1950-55	18.9	—3.9	—0.7	18.2	—0.8	13.0
Sweden						
12. 1861-90	9.2	—34.1	—3.3	5.9	—3.4	2.2
13. 1881-1910	15.0	—24.5	—3.4	11.7	—3.6	5.7
14. 1901-30	19.8	—1.4	—0.2	19.6	—0.2	12.5
15. 1950-55	20.5	2.9	0.6	21.1	n.a.	n.a.
Italy						
16. 1861-90	10.1	—13.2	—1.4	8.8	—1.5	3.6
17. 1881-1913	12.5	2.7	0.3	12.8	0.3	7.0
18. 1921-40	16.8	—8.3	—1.4	15.4	—1.5	7.4
19. 1951-55	20.3	—11.7	—2.4	17.9	—2.6	9.9

Table 9 (Cont'd)—Long-Term Changes in Proportions of Capital Formation and Net Movements in Foreign Claims to Domestic or National Product; Selected Countries (Based on Totals in Current Prices)

	(1)	(2)	(3)	(4)	(5)	(6)
U.S.A.						
20. 1869-98	21.9	—2.5	—0.5	21.4	—0.6	13.5
21. 1899-1928	20.5	8.4	1.7	22.2	1.9	12.7
22. 1919-48	21.3	4.8	1.0	22.3	1.2	8.7
23. 1950-55	18.1	2.8	0.5	18.6	0.6	11.1
Canada[b] (excluding inventories)						
24. 1901-30	20.3	—20.0	—5.0	15.3	—5.5	9.3
25. 1921-50	16.0	5.7	0.8	16.8	0.9	8.2
26. 1950-55	22.3	—7.5	—1.7	20.6	—1.9	12.0
Argentina[c] (excluding inventories) Ratio to domestic product						
27. 1900-29	31.5	—33.0	—10.4	21.1	—11.7	11.0
28. 1925-54	24.0	—8.8	—2.1	21.9	—2.5	6.5
29. 1950-54	22.5	—3.1	—0.7	21.8	—0.8	8.0

For all countries except Italy and Argentina, the data for pre-World War II years are from Simon Kuznets, "International Differences in Capital Formation and Financing," Moses Abramovitz (ed.), *Capital Formation and Economic Growth* (Princeton, N. J.: Princeton University Press for the National Bureau of Economic Research, 1956), pp. 19-111, particularly Tables I-3 and II-4; the data for post-World War II years are from the United Nations source cited in the notes to Table 8. The data for Italy are from "Indagine Statistica sullo Aviluppo del Reddito Nazionale dell' Italia del 1861 al 1956," *Annali di Statistica*, Ser. VIII, Vol. IX (Rome, 1957). The data for Argentina are from the paper by Mr. Ganz cited in the notes to Table 2.

In general, the ratios for the long periods before World War II were calculated from ratios for decade intervals by simple unweighted averaging. The only weighting used was to allow, if needed, for different durations of periods combined into a single longer time span.

a. The Cairncross-Lenfant estimates of net changes in foreign claims were used here.

b. The Buckley and Firestone estimates of capital formation (both excluding inventories) were combined directly, without any adjustment for the minor lack of comparability.

c. The estimate of net changes in claim against foreign countries is identical with what Mr. Ganz described as foreign fixed capital investment. Conceptually, the two totals are different, but over long periods the discrepancy between the two must be relatively slight.

rises, whereas in others, e.g., the United States and Denmark, no such rises are observed. In most of the countries the ratio of net capital formation to net national product declines, but not in the United Kingdom, Italy, or Sweden. And there are divergent movements in the ratio of gross domestic capital formation to gross national product (the latter is fairly close to gross domestic product for which no long-term estimates are available). Clearly, the sample is far too small to give us firm findings on a rather varied set of trends that apparently characterize capital formation proportions. It is probably safer to advance some reasonable conjectures, rather than rely on the findings in Table 9—although the latter have some suggestive value.

a) First, there is likely to be a difference between young and "empty" countries, like the United States, Canada, and Argentina, and the five older countries in Table 9. Given a minimum of political stability and security, the young countries may have quite high ratios of domestic capital formation to national product even in early periods of growth before industrialization, and given the relatively high per capita income levels, even the national capital formation proportions may be high. The coming of industrialization *may* raise the capital formation proportions somewhat, but such a rise is far from inevitable or even probable. By contrast, in countries with a long pre-industrial history of low per capita income and low capital formation proportions, there is likely to be a rise in the capital formation proportions, with a shift to the industrial system. The same would be true of those young countries in which there had been prolonged political instability, and the levels of economic performance and capital formation proportions had, as a result, been kept down. Thus, in the earlier

periods of economic growth one may find relatively constant capital formation proportions in some countries and
rising trends in others—whether the proportions are gross
or net, domestic or national. Indeed, in some, domestic
capital proportions may decline, as suggested by the estimates for Argentina—although here, because I am not
familiar with the data and with the country's economic
history, my comment is more of a question than a positive
statement.

b) Among the *follower* countries, i.e., those that enter
the period of industrialization and modern economic growth
later than others, a substantial part of domestic capital
formation is likely to be financed at first by foreign capital funds. This would be particularly true if the country is
small in relation to the potential lenders on the world capital markets (observe the high negative ratios of net changes
in foreign claims to domestic capital formation, in the
early periods in Sweden, Canada, and Argentina). As development proceeds, the debtor position is likely to be
reduced and eventually the countries may shift to a cred-
itor position. These are familiar trends. Perhaps less familiar
are the reverse trends in countries that entered the period
of industrialization before the others and became the world
creditors. The slowing down of their rates of growth and
the loss in relative position, accentuated by wars (even if
the countries were among the "victors"), may bring about
a sharp reduction in the volume of foreign investment relative to total national savings and capital formation. The
drop by 1950-55 in the share of foreign capital investment
for the United Kingdom is probably not a historical accident but part of a long-term trend.

c) The long-term constancy of the national gross capital

formation proportions has attracted attention since it has been observed in countries like the United States (and several others) where growth in real per capita income has been substantial. This constancy, despite the great rise in real income, is in sharp contrast with the cross-section analysis in which high income levels within a country are associated with high net or gross savings proportions. This is not the place to deal with this problem, on which so much ink and hypothesizing have already been expended, except to say that there is no hard and fast connection between *any* cross-section relation at a given point of time within a country and the relation between secular trends over time. By definition, the whole context within which cross-section relations are observed changes in the course of time. Consumption patterns as well as savings patterns change in response to technological changes and higher income levels; while it is possible, with higher per capita income levels, to save larger proportions without worsening material well-being, there is no inherent compulsion to do so. Furthermore, many factors affected by secular changes —e.g., the shift away from the savings-oriented individual entrepreneurship toward employee status and investment in human training and skills, and the narrowing of inequality in the size distribution of income—may work toward *declining* rather than constant gross capital formation proportions.

d) Given constant gross capital formation proportions and retardation in the rate of growth of gross national product (of the type suggested in Table 4), there will be retardation also in the rate of growth of gross capital formation (measured in volumes in constant prices). Given the latter, there will be, other conditions being equal, a rise in the ratio of capital consumption charges to gross capital formation: the former are in a sense cumulations of *past* volumes of capital investment, and if the past volumes were growing at higher rates than current volumes, the ratio of the former to the latter will increase. Thus, given a constant life span of fixed capital, subject to capital consumption charges, and a constant ratio of depreciable capital components (fixed capital) to non-depreciable (net changes in inventories and in foreign claims), retardation in the rate of growth of gross capital formation means a rise in the ratio of capital consumption charges (depreciation) to current gross capital formation. With such a rise, constancy or even a slight rise in gross capital formation proportions will necessarily mean a decline in net capital formation proportions; this is the reason for the downward trend in net capital formation proportions, and not in the gross capital formation proportions, in several countries, in Table 9. The difference in trends in the developed countries also reflects the shift after a while, within fixed capital formation, away from the longer-lived construction toward the shorter-lived machinery and equipment. This shift reduces the weighted average life span of fixed capital subject to depreciation, thus raising even further the ratio of depreciation to gross capital formation, and adds to the decline in the share of net capital formation in net national product.

One implication of these trends should be noted. Capital consumption charges in the developed countries are heavily concentrated in the hands of business corporations and are a way of financing gross capital formation. The rise in the share of capital consumption charges in gross capital formation means, therefore, a rise in the proportion that can be financed by funds earned and retained by corporations; there is, of course, the additional source in the retained net profits of corporations that grow proportionately with the increasing weight of the corporate sector in the economy. The trends that have been discussed, therefore, reflect shifts in the structure of financing, at least in the private sector of the developed economies. There are, certainly, numerous other shifts in the financing of capital formation, but these are not revealed or even suggested in Table 9.

e) The trends in capital formation proportions noted above relate to capital limited to material investment, excluding investment in human beings represented by growth-promoting components of consumer or government expenditures. For this wider concept of capital, some of the long-term trends might look quite different. Very likely, the proportions of capital formation, including investment in human beings, to national product in the developed economies would not be constant or decline, but would instead show sustained rises. Incidentally, the long-term association between the rise in income and savings proportions would then be reconciled with the cross-section relation between level of income and the savings ratios. Any exploration of the trends of capital formation geared to this wider definition requires prolonged empirical study and reformulation of analytical concepts, both still in the future.

Lecture V

THE PROBLEM OF SIZE

WE HAVE DISCUSSED various aspects of the economic growth of nations, treating the latter as equivalent units regardless of size. For the statistical tables in particular *unweighted* averages of the measures for each country were computed, which means that all countries were given equal weight regardless of the size of their population and national product. A question may legitimately be raised as to whether this approach is justified, since it implies that there is no significant relation between the size of a country and its economic growth.

The question acquires more importance when we recognize the vast differences in size among nations. Even if we omit splinter units whose political independence is more a matter of historical curiosity than of real significance, even if we exclude, as we did, countries whose population was less than a million in recent years, the range is still extremely wide. On the one hand, we have states with a few million inhabitants, like Norway, Sweden, Denmark, Switzerland, and on the other hand, we have giant states like China, India, the U.S.S.R., and the United States, with 170 million or more inhabitants. Not only is the range in the distribution by size wide, but the distribution is skewed. According to data in W. S. and E. J. Woytinsky, *World Commerce and Governments* (Twentieth Century Fund, 1955; Tables 194 and 196, pp. 564-66), of a total of between 80 and 90 states (excluding such splinters as Monaco, Andorra, Luxembourg, etc.), the four largest account for well over half of the world's population. At the other extreme, 47 states, each with a population of 10 million or less, account for less than 8 per cent of the world's population. Can one hope to establish significant general features of modern economic growth by treating Sweden and the United States, Ceylon and India, or Honduras and Brazil as comparable and equivalent units?

My answer to this question, as a *first* approximation, is in the affirmative. In so far as modern economic growth is a combination of the industrial system, a community of human wants, and an organization of mankind in sovereign states, the modern economic growth of Sweden and the United States should be expected to show many common features: a shift from agriculture toward other sectors in the economy; a shift from family and individual firms toward corporations; similar trends in the capital formation proportions; and so on. In so far as Ceylon and India are both basically agricultural economies, little affected by modern industrialization and with the typically excessive ratios of population to land (under the prevailing patterns of domestic technology), their economic structures and their patterns of growth should also display considerable similarity—regardless of the wide difference in size. If any further proof is needed that size of a country is not the crucial determinant of economic growth as reflected in per capita income (or any other index), a brief reference to the easily available measures will suffice. Among the large nations we have one that is most advanced, the United States (in group I) and two that are among the most underdeveloped, India and China (both in group VII); among the middle-size nations, with a population between twenty and a hundred million, we have highly developed units like the United Kingdom and Germany (the former in group I and the latter in group II), as well as underdeveloped units like Pakistan, Indonesia, and Egypt (all in group VII); among the small nations, with a population of less than 10 million, we have highly developed units like Sweden and Switzerland (both in group I) and those well down the scale like Ceylon, Haiti, and Paraguay.

This does not mean that the size of a nation has no effect on *some* aspects of economic growth and on *some* institutional changes and policy problems encountered. It only means that size, in and of itself, is not so crucial that it must be included as a dominant factor in any initial review and discussion of characteristics of modern economic growth. Yet size is of some effect; while its bearing upon economic growth cannot be discussed fully here, partly for lack of time but largely for lack of work on the problem, some of the more obvious lines of connection can be suggested. By discussion in terms of the very small nations or the very large, i.e., by using the extreme values in the range, we can bring out the possible effects of size most sharply. We prefer to consider the small nations—for present purposes, units with less than 10 million population—since there are quite a number of them in the world today. The dividing line is necessarily arbitrary, but it is convenient to have one. The arguments adduced will be more or less potent, as the dividing line is drawn further down or further up the scale of population size.

a) Other conditions being equal, the economic structure of a small nation will be less diversified than that of a larger unit—production will be more concentrated in fewer industrial sectors (defined broadly to include all branches of productive activity). There are several reasons for greater concentration of industrial structure in small nations. First, the latter usually have an appreciably smaller territory than the large, and diversity of natural resources is to a large extent a function of area size. Larger nations with larger areas are likely to have diversity of underground resources, land surface, water bodies, coastlines, and climate. Each smaller nation may have much less varied natural conditions. Second, the minimum scale of a plant, let alone the optimum, for some modern industries could be sustained by the economy of a small nation only at a loss or on the basis of foreign markets (consider production of airplanes, automobiles, heavy electrical generators, and the like). Foreign markets are rarely a sound basis for developing domestic industries, and there is a limit to the economic loss that can be sustained even for the sake of having some important industries inside the boundaries or for the sake of national prestige. Third, each small nation may have *some* advantage, either in the way of natural resources (e.g., the oil fields of the Arab states), or in the way of location (e.g., Switzerland today or Venice in the past). Given such an advantage vis-à-vis worldwide markets, a large proportion of a small nation's limited capital and labor power may be concentrated in one or a few sectors. A large nation can divide its greater volume of resources among a greater number of sectors with potential comparative advantage.

b) At a given level of per capita economic performance, the broad structure of final demand (flow of goods to consumers and capital formation) is likely to be the same for a small and a large nation. It will be equally diversified for both in the sense that even though the small nation does not produce its own automobiles, it will still demand them if its per capita income warrants such expenditures, and even though the resources of some Arab states, for example, are so engrossed in production of crude oil that they cannot produce their own food and clothing, they will demand the latter at levels appropriate to their per capita income. It follows that, at comparable levels of per capita economic performance, the disparity between the diversified structure of final demand and the more concentrated structure of domestic product will be proportionately far greater for small nations than for large.

c) This disparity is, of course, made possible by foreign trade. It is through imports that the final demand of a country, more diversified than domestic production, can be fully satisfied, and it is the exports of the excess product of some more developed domestic sectors that pay for the imports. It follows that foreign trade must be more important relative to total output for smaller than for larger countries. Moreover, the markets of smaller nations, with smaller areas, are more exposed to foreign competition than those of larger nations, with larger territories. A large territory means that a large part of final demand within the country is well away from its boundaries, and domestic producers in large nations therefore have a natural advantage because of differential transportation costs.

That the proportion of foreign trade to total product is much greater in small countries than in large is clearly shown in Table 10. The foreign trade ratio for each country was calculated by dividing the sum of commodity exports and imports by the sum of national income and imports (all in current prices). The proper numerator should have included exports and imports of services; the proper denominator should have been the sum of gross national product and imports of all goods. But these are not easily available, and the differences among countries shown by the latter would be quite similar to those actually summarized in Table 10. As in all other tables, the group entries are unweighted arithmetic means of the ratios calculated separately for each country.

In the extreme case where there would be no imports or exports, the ratio would obviously be 0. At the other extreme, if there were no domestic production and only imports, and obviously no exports (which in this case would be only re-exports), the ratio would be 1.0. If imports were equal to domestic output (as measured by national income), and exports were equal to imports, the ratio would be 1.0. With exports equal to imports, a ratio of 0.2 means that imports are somewhat over a tenth of national product; a ratio of 0.4 means that imports are 0.25 of national product.

When the countries are grouped by size of population, the foreign trade ratio rises as we go down the scale—from less than, or close to, 0.2 to close to, or over, 0.4. If we were to group countries by per capita income within each size group, the same inverse association between size (measured by population) and the foreign trade ratio would be found. Size in this case is a far more important variable than per capita income. When, as in the lower panel of Table 10, countries are grouped by per capita income, ignoring population size, no systematic change in the foreign trade ratios is found as we move down the income scale. And the same lack of association would persist if we were to subdivide the groups by population size. In other words, even at comparable size levels, higher per capita income levels are not necessarily accompanied by higher foreign trade ratios. The possible reasons for this lack of association are suggested below.

d) Two other distinctive characteristics of the foreign trade of small nations should be noted. First, the exports are more likely to be concentrated in one or two commodities than in the case of the larger nations, especially in the less developed countries whose exports are in worldwide demand (oil, coffee, tin, etc.). However, this concentration of exports may extend even to the larger underdeveloped countries, where low level technology affords comparative advantage to only a limited range of goods. Second, imports and particularly exports of small nations are likely to be concentrated with respect to country of destination or origin—large proportions of total exports going to one large country, and large proportions of imports coming from it. Larger countries are likely to export to and import from a larger number of countries.

e) Foreign trade, in general, serves as a mechanism of international division of labor, permitting specialization in production in different countries and exchange of products among them. For these reasons foreign trade is far more important for small nations than for the larger units, since it offsets the limitations that would otherwise be imposed on their final consumption by the greater concentration of their domestic productive structure. But it is unlikely that small nations can fully offset the disadvantages of size through the instrumentality of foreign trade, since foreign trade is not free and reliable at all times. In the

Table 10—Relation between Foreign Commodity Trade, Size of Country, and Level of Income Per Capita, 1938-39 and 1950-54

GROUPS OF COUNTRIES		Number of Countries (1)	1938-39 Average Population (millions) or Average Income Per Capita ($) (2)	Average Foreign Trade Ratio (3)	Number of Countries (4)	1950-54 Average Population (millions) or Average Income Per Capita ($) (5)	Average Foreign Trade Ratio (6)
A.	**Countries Arrayed in Descending Order of Population Size**						
1.	I	10	135.4	0.17	10	103.9	0.21
2.	II	10	16.2	0.24	10	22.0	0.24
3	III	10	7.3	0.31	10	10.4	0.41
4	IV	10	3.7	0.38	10	5.3	0.41
5	V	12	1.5	0.38	10	2.7	0.41
6.	VI				7	0.8	0.41
B.	**Countries Arrayed in Descending Order of Income Per Capita**						
7.	I	10	429	0.29	10	1,021	0.35
8	II	10	214	0.32	10	514	0.41
9	III	10	106	0.29	10	291	0.40
10.	IV	10	66	0.36	10	200	0.24
11.	V	12	40	0.24	10	115	0.38
12.	VI				7	67	0.26

All data in this table and in Table 11 are from an unpublished doctoral dissertation submitted in 1958 at the Johns Hopkins University by Mr. Rolf R. Piekarz, entitled "Proportion of Foreign Trade in National Product and Economic Growth." They were taken by Mr. Piekarz from the standard sources on foreign trade, and from the well-known sources on national product and population.

The foreign trade ratios in columns 3 and 6 are based on the ratios for individual countries. The ratio of imports and exports in current prices to national income plus imports (total availability) was calculated and then the ratios for the separate countries were averaged (unweighted arithmetic means) for the successive groups of countries in the arrays.

The ratios in column 3 are of foreign trade in 1938 to the sum of national income in 1939 and imports in 1938—national income estimates being readily available for 1939, and 1938 being a preferable year for imports and exports in order to exclude the effects upon them of the initiation of World War II. The ratios in column 6 are of average imports and exports for 1950-54 to average national income plus imports for 1950-54.

The countries are limited to politically independent states. No colonies are included.

world as it is, foreign trade not only has to meet its "normal" costs, but it can also be disturbed by governmental intervention and by international conflicts, overt or covert. Consequently small nations tend to foster domestic industries which, because of the narrow domestic market, cannot be as efficient as those in the larger nations with their wider domestic markets. Furthermore, some essential goods cannot be moved across a nation's boundaries except at excessive and truly prohibitive costs. Some of these were suggested above in the attempt to explain the large share of the S sector in all countries. One cannot import or export (except in small part) the construction, transportation, communication, and retail distribution services within a country; or the professional and personal services; or the predominant part of government services. Many of these activities, the production of many commodities, are subject to economies of scale; and it may well be that in many small countries the maximum efficiency to which such activities can be raised, given the limited internal market, is far lower than in the larger nations.

Some hint of the limits to which foreign trade can be pressed to supplement the specialization of productive structure in small nations is given in Table 10. The rise in the average foreign trade ratio associated with a decline in the size of population ceases once this ratio reaches certain high levels. Thus for 1938-39 the highest ratio, 0.38, is reached in group IV with an average population of close to 4 million, and the ratio remains the same in the next group, even though average population drops to 1.5 million. The evidence of a limit is even stronger in 1950-54: the ratio reaches its maximum, 0.41, in group III with a population average of about 10.5 million, and is no higher even in the group with an average population per country of less than 1 million. Apparently, under prevailing political, institutional, and economic conditions the proportion of total available product that can be secured from foreign trade has an upper limit, and the proportion of output that must be secured from sources within the domestic boundaries has a corresponding lower limit.

f) The preceding comments suggest that despite the international division of labor permitted and fostered by foreign trade, small nations may suffer from inefficiency of size, in that some activities that must be pursued within their boundaries cannot take full advantage of the economies of scale possible for larger countries. The magnitude of the resulting inefficiency and the sectors of the productive structure that it affects most, are important questions in the study of economic growth, but they cannot be answered without data on the costs and returns of comparable lines of production among nations that differ mainly in size.

Granted diseconomies of scale, and hence obstacles to economic growth in small nations, there must also be some offsetting advantages—since many small nations are now among the most developed, whereas many large nations are at low levels of per capita economic performance and have not yet adopted the industrial system. These advantages are elusive and difficult to demonstrate by objective evidence. One major benefit of small size must lie in the internal unity that can be attained, and hence in the ease with which decisions basic to successful economic growth can be made. To be sure, some small nations are struggling with recalcitrant and deviant minorities, and are less unified than some large countries (comparison of

Lebanon with the United States easily comes to mind). However, among the small nations there are many in which linguistic, cultural, and other unity are at high levels, higher levels perhaps than are attainable in the large countries, in which regional diversities are inconspicuous, and in which minorities, if they exist, count for little. Under such conditions, it is relatively easy to make secular decisions—on land tenure, labor problems, control of business enterprises, taxation, and so on down the line. These decisions, always affecting some groups favorably and others adversely and acted upon in the belief that they contribute to the long-term growth and welfare of the country as a whole, are far easier when there is a strong sense of community in the population and when they can be made by democratic means rather than by dictatorial ukase. Obviously, community of feeling, a sense of common destiny, and subordination of individual or group interest to that of the whole, are far easier to attain in small and homogeneous nations than in the larger nations with their regional, racial, and other diversities. Even the United States has a problem in the South and a conflict between eastern and western groups, and one need not stress the diversities in India, Indonesia, Pakistan, among the large underdeveloped countries, or in France, among the large developed countries.

Another possible advantage of small units is the rapidity with which they can adjust to changing situations. In a sense this rapidity is related to the greater possible ease of reaching secular decisions. For slowness in adjusting may be due to the disparate effect that changes may have upon different groups within the country, and to the resistance of some to the proper adaptation to the change.

A greater community of feeling thus not only helps to make the necessary decisions but also permits them to be made promptly. And since economic growth is a process of continuous adjustment to a changing technological potential and a changing constellation of national structures, the speed with which small nations may be able to make such an adjustment is a great advantage.

TRENDS IN
FOREIGN TRADE RATIOS

If size is inversely correlated with the ratio of foreign trade to national output (or availability, i.e., product plus imports), as the cross-section data in Table 10 indicate, the increase in the size of a country accompanying economic growth should mean, other conditions being equal, a downward trend in the foreign trade ratio. But no such declining trend is observed in Table 11 which includes long-term estimates for ten countries.

Despite the fact that the table omits war periods when trade flows are naturally distorted, and even if we disregard some other exceptional periods, like the decade of the 1930's that was dominated by the great depression, there is no prevalence of trends in one direction. In some countries for which records extend far back, e.g., Sweden, Japan, the United Kingdom, and France, the foreign trade ratio rises and then declines. In others—the Netherlands and the United States—the trend is on the whole downward, even though in the United States the record goes as

Table 11—Long-Term Changes in the Ratio of Foreign Commodity Trade to National Income Plus Imports; Selected Countries

COUNTRY AND PERIOD	IMPORT RATIO (1)	EXPORT RATIO (2)	FOREIGN TRADE RATIO (3)
United Kingdom			
1. 1831, 1836, 1841	0.12	0.09	0.21
2. 1841, 1846, 1851	0.14	0.11	0.25
3. 1851, 1860	0.16	0.13	0.29
4. 1860, 1867, 1870	0.23	0.16	0.39
5. 1870-79	0.26	0.20	0.46
6. 1880-89	0.29	0.26	0.55
7. 1890-99	0.24	0.16	0.40
8. 1900-09	0.24	0.17	0.41
9. 1920-29	0.23	0.17	0.40
10. 1930-39	0.17	0.10	0.27
11. 1945-52	0.18	0.14	0.32
France			
12. 1841-50	0.08	0.08	0.16
13. 1851-60	0.12	0.13	0.25
14. 1861-70	0.15	0.16	0.31
15. 1871-80	0.16	0.15	0.31
16. 1881-90	0.18	0.15	0.33
17. 1891-1900	0.15	0.15	0.30
18. 1901-10	0.17	0.16	0.33
19. 1920-28	0.28	0.21	0.49
20. 1929-38	0.14	0.10	0.24
21. 1946-51	0.15	0.10	0.25
Netherlands			
22. 1900-08	0.56	0.46	1.01
23. 1909-18	0.47	0.38	0.85
24. 1919-28	0.31	0.20	0.51
25. 1929-38	0.24	0.17	0.41
26. 1944-53	0.34	0.25	0.59
27. 1950-54	0.35	0.28	0.62
Denmark			
28. 1870-78	0.24	0.19	0.43
29. 1879-88	0.26	0.19	0.44
30. 1889-98	0.28	0.21	0.49
31. 1899-1908	0.31	0.25	0.57
32. 1909-18	0.25	0.22	0.47
33. 1919-28	0.26	0.21	0.47
34. 1929-38	0.22	0.18	0.40
35. 1944-53	0.20	0.17	0.37
36. 1950-54	0.25	0.20	0.45

Table 11 (Cont'd)—Long-Term Changes in the Ratio of Foreign Commodity Trade to National Income Plus Imports; Selected Countries

COUNTRY AND PERIOD	IMPORT RATIO (1)	EXPORT RATIO (2)	FOREIGN TRADE RATIO (3)
Norway			
37. 1900-08	0.21	0.14	0.35
38. 1909-18	0.24	0.15	0.39
39. 1919-28	0.23	0.12	0.35
40. 1929-38	0.16	0.12	0.28
41. 1946-53	0.22	0.13	0.34
42. 1950-54	0.22	0.14	0.36
Sweden			
43. 1861-68	0.12	0.11	0.22
44. 1869-78	0.17	0.14	0.31
45. 1879-88	0.19	0.15	0.35
46. 1889-98	0.19	0.16	0.35
47. 1899-1908	0.19	0.14	0.33
48. 1909-18	0.15	0.17	0.32
49. 1919-28	0.16	0.14	0.30
50. 1929-38	0.14	0.13	0.27
51. 1939-48	0.12	0.09	0.21
52. 1944-53	0.15	0.13	0.28
53. 1950-54	0.17	0.13	0.30
Italy			
54. 1864-73	0.11	0.09	0.20
55. 1874-83	0.12	0.11	0.22
56. 1884-93	0.12	0.08	0.20
57. 1894-1903	0.12	0.10	0.22
58. 1904-13	0.15	0.11	0.26
59. 1919-28	0.15	0.09	0.25
60. 1929-38	0.20	0.07	0.27
61. 1944-53	0.16	0.11	0.27
62. 1949-54	0.13	0.09	0.21
United States			
63. 1869-78	0.07	0.07	0.14
64. 1879-88	0.06	0.07	0.13
65. 1889-98	0.05	0.07	0.13
66. 1899-1908	0.05	0.07	0.12
67. 1909-18	0.05	0.09	0.14
68. 1919-28	0.05	0.07	0.12
69. 1929-38	0.04	0.04	0.08
70. 1944-53	0.04	0.06	0.11
71. 1950-53	0.04	0.06	0.10

Table 11 (Cont'd)—Long-Term Changes in the Ratio of Foreign Commodity Trade to National Income Plus Imports; Selected Countries

COUNTRY AND PERIOD	IMPORT RATIO (1)	EXPORT RATIO (2)	FOREIGN TRADE RATIO (3)
Canada			
72. 1870-79	0.20	0.15	0.34
73. 1880-89	0.15	0.14	0.29
74. 1890-99	0.12	0.13	0.25
75. 1900-09	0.19	0.17	0.36
76. 1910-19	0.21	0.23	0.44
77. 1920-29	0.15	0.17	0.32
78. 1930-39	0.12	0.14	0.26
79. 1945-54	0.15	0.16	0.31
80. 1950-54	0.15	0.15	0.30
Japan			
81. 1878-87	0.05	0.06	0.11
82. 1888-97	0.09	0.09	0.18
83. 1898-1907	0.13	0.11	0.25
84. 1908-17	0.13	0.15	0.29
85. 1918-27	0.15	0.13	0.28
86. 1928-37	0.14	0.13	0.27
87. 1950-54	0.12	0.08	0.20

For sources and general procedure see the notes to Table 10.

In general, for the decade or other period averages, imports, exports, and national income were averaged and ratios of averages calculated.

The entries in lines 1-4 are averages of data for the years indicated.

far back as the 1870's. In still others—Denmark, Norway, Canada, Italy—the ratio is relatively constant, although punctuated by deviations in some decades. Apparently, as in many other aspects of economic activity, the cross-section relation does not hold over the long run. Nor is this surprising since the trend is affected by a wide variety of secularly changing factors whose different combinations produce different movements for different countries in different periods.

The forces that determine trends in the foreign trade

ratio, even for the developed countries (no others are included in Table 11), are complex and varied. To begin with, technological changes in transportation and communication, as well as new economic and institutional devices, must continuously facilitate movements across boundaries, i.e., make for substantial rises in the absolute volume of foreign trade. However, this does not necessarily mean rises in the foreign trade *ratio,* since the same changes also facilitate *internal* trade, and they and related innovations make for rising volumes of total product (i.e., of the denominator of the ratio). Thus, for some countries and for some periods the trend in the foreign trade ratio may be upward, and for others downward, because in the former the foreign trade-inducing technological and associated changes outweigh the others; whereas in the latter, technology furthers internal trade more and thus diverts an increasing part of domestic output into domestic markets.

Second, some phases in the development of the industrial structures of countries may further foreign trade more than others, hence raising the foreign trade ratio in one period and reducing it in another. Thus, when the M sector is developing more rapidly (accompanied by sharp increases in productivity of the A sector) than the S sector, the foreign trade ratio may rise, other conditions being equal. In the phase in which an increasing share of the output is moving into the S sector, the foreign trade ratio may decline, or at least fail to rise.

Third, the constellation of diverse structures of national economies, which are the units in the network of international commodity trade, changes over time. Some of the shifts, particularly those precipitated by world conflicts, may be quite sharp. The very change in the number of independent states that become "foreign" to each other would presumably affect the volume and weight of international or foreign trade relative to domestic trade or domestic output—so that political consolidation would, other conditions being equal, result in declining trends in the foreign trade ratio, and political fragmentation would presumably have the opposite effect. Even more important are the possible changes in national policies with reference to foreign trade. A shift in the identity of the economic leader nation from one that, like the United Kingdom, sought to further free international trade to those that, like the United States and Germany, developed under the aegis of protective tariffs, was in itself important. And the emergence recently of authoritarian states that combine forced industrialization with economic isolation and strict controls over foreign trade and other movements across boundaries, was obviously a major factor in the decline in the ratio of foreign trade to total world output, as well as in the lower level of the foreign trade ratio for many countries in post-World War I and post-World War II years. Finally, wars themselves, disrupting the customary channels of trade, are a retarding factor regardless of changes in policy on the part of the authoritarian members in the concert of nations.

The list of factors suggested is far from exhaustive but long enough to "explain," by judicious combination, the rising trends of the foreign trade ratio for some countries and periods, the constant trends for other countries and periods, and the declining trends for still others. Such *ad hoc* use of various hypotheses out of a capacious grab bag would be helpful only if we could, by empirical checks, identify in advance the specific factors and study their incidence at a given period and in a given country. The few such checks at hand do not suffice for the purpose.

Nevertheless, Table 11 and the general comments suggested by it are useful in two ways. First, they stress the fact that foreign trade-flows and other movements across national boundaries are affected by many complex factors, in which technological changes, social inventions, economic advantages, political revolutions, and diversities in the structures and endowment of nations all play their part; it may be that economic advantages do not play a truly dominant role. Consequently, there is a wide gap between the trends in foreign trade observed in reality and static international trade theory, i.e., international trade models that could be derived from some assumptions concerning economic growth patterns of members of the trading community. This is hardly an unexpected conclusion but it may be worth repeating in view of the facility with which generalizations are advanced in this field.

The second conclusion stresses the variability over time of the foreign trade ratios. Most of the entries in Table 11 are decade averages and are presumably free from most, if not all, cyclical and short-term fluctuations. Nevertheless, the export ratio for the United Kingdom doubled in thirty years, from the mid-1850's to the mid-1880's (from 0.13 to 0.26), and then declined in a decade to about six-tenths of its peak value. These ratios are close approximations to the income propensities to import and export, widely used in model-building analysis and in projections; it is clear that these propensities which vary sensitively in the short run are also far from stable secularly. Until we know more about the secular movements and the factors that determine them, there is always the danger of confusing them with short-term responses. In consequence, much of the current analysis and work on projections may turn out to have been built on shifting sands.

Lecture VI

THE TASKS OF THEORY

THE DISCUSSION ABOVE of selected aspects of modern economic growth of nations is a partial summary of a detailed study still in progress. The study aims at establishing the similar and disparate characteristics of growth, in its impact on the initially different economic structures of nations over as much of the world as the readily available quantitative data permit. We could extend the list of characteristics summarized, or subject some of those already noted to a more detailed or different analysis, but I prefer to discuss the theoretical goals toward which the study is oriented. In this way both the broader characteristics of modern economic growth and some of the more detailed findings will be seen within a wider intellectual framework and perspective—always a useful approach when one studies a complex and variegated process of change.

a) The major guiding assumption is, of course, that modern economic growth has many generally observed characteristics by which the process can be identified and which warrant the expectation of finding a number of common aspects interrelated in sufficiently coherent and invariant fashion to amount to more than a mere statistical generalization or mechanical coincidence. Thus, in speaking of modern economic growth as the adoption of the industrial system, we imply that the system—a potential possession of all mankind—is in many essential respects one and the same thing in the free or mixed economies of western Europe, in some of its offshoots overseas, in Japan, and in an authoritarian state like the U.S.S.R. In all of these, it means the applications to problems of production of modern scientific discoveries and additions to the stock of tested knowledge. In all of these it requires a minimum of common social concomitants: it cannot be applied without a minimum level of literacy and skill on the part of the population; the technological conditions of its economies of scale require a shift from the personal or familial type of organization of the productive unit to the impersonal and bureaucratic (represented by corporations, private or public); and the very sequence of its application within a country necessitates a certain order of development. For example, efficient transportation and communication must be attained before far-reaching division of labor within a country can become a reality and before the producing enterprises can enjoy the indispensable external economies.

Furthermore, because the industrial system is adopted by communities of human beings whose structures of wants and aspirations are similar, the rise in per worker productivity and in per capita income that follows the adoption of the industrial system is accompanied by a number of other general features. To mention a few, there are the changes in demographic patterns due to the effects of high level technology on the birth and death rates; the shift away from agriculture, so widely noted that the whole process is called "industrialization"; the associated process of urbanization, a complex of far-reaching changes in the whole pattern of societies undergoing modern economic growth; and the change in the scale of social values, particularly in the weight of economic values relative to those derived from non-economic and traditional sources. All these patterns and trends are observable in *all* societies that experience modern economic growth—capitalist and communist, libertarian and authoritarian, western and eastern.

Finally, the industrial system spreads in a world organized in sovereign political units, and it is reasonable to argue that some minimum of political independence and of coherence and efficiency in the structure of the state are indispensable prerequisites for effective modern economic growth. This, with its various obvious ramifications, constitutes another common element that we should expect to find.

Many other general features could probably be added, but it is neither necessary nor possible to be exhaustive. What we have said is sufficient to indicate that the first task of theory in the field is the formulation of the essential and common aspects of modern economic growth and the analysis of their interrelations—a testable model that would weave the common elements of the industrial system, the structure of human wants and aspirations, and the political and social concomitants, into a unified whole. In so doing, it would be incorrect to assume that all these common, transnational forces, as it were, are a fixed set that does not itself change over time. The complex of technological change and scientific knowledge that underlies the industrial system has changed greatly from its early state in the second half of the eighteenth century in Great Britain. The structure of human wants and aspirations has also been evolving under the impact of the changing potential of technical and economic progress and of the spreading change in outlook that greater economic attainment has itself brought about. The functions of the state, particularly in relation to the other organizational structures within society, and resulting in part from economic growth, have also been changing over time. A general model of the industrial system with its minimum political and social concomitants, cannot, therefore, be static, but must provide for analysis of the factors that determine the trends in the system, permitting us to distinguish between the persistent and the transient, between the elements of order and those of historical accident or contingency.

b) The industrial system and its social concomitants, as suggested above, are a formalized, ideal-type construct, reflecting a major innovation which has actually occurred (and is still occurring) within a specific historical epoch. We set its beginning at the mid-eighteenth century, knowing full well that the question of the initial date has been and will continue to be the subject of much erudite and enlightening discussion. Whatever the initial date, the point is that the industrial system, coming, as it did, late in a long history, emerged and spread in a world of nation-states (or political units akin to them) that had widely different structures and antecedent history. Consequently, those cases of modern economic growth that we can observe, measure, and analyze, cannot be treated as simple combinations of the industrial system and its concomitants, either with a *tabula rasa* or with a sprinkling of random, stochastically treatable variables. On the contrary, each represents a distinctive complex of natural and historical endowments, and differs substantially from others in size, resources, location, and particularly in the structure of social and economic institutions inherited from the past. Hence, the observable cases of modern economic growth are best viewed as combinations of the industrial system (including its minimum social concomitants) with the distinctive initial structure of each country involved. Where such modern economic growth has in fact taken place, the general pattern set by the industrial system can be said to have been only modified, but not significantly inhibited, by each country's initial structure and position. Where economic growth has been limited or hardly begun, the initial structure may also have been affected but in essentially different ways.

With the basic model formulated, the second task of theory is to analyze and formalize the effects of different initial structures of nation-states upon the patterns of economic growth that ensued, and upon characteristics of the mature economies in which modern development has been attained. The emphasis here is on the differences in the patterns of modern economic growth and in the resulting structures, rather than upon their common characteristics. But these differences must be associated with some generally formulatable conditions, not treated as historical accidents. Illustrations of this sort of analysis were provided in some of the discussion above, e.g., when we dealt with differences between the growth patterns of the young and "empty" countries and the old and "full" countries, and in the discussion of the degree of reliance upon foreign trade and other distinctions between small and large nations.

Clearly, if the range of differences in initial structure of nations is extended far enough, there will be cases in which the emergence and impact of the industrial system will *not* result in its adoption—countries that have failed, in varying degree, to follow successfully the pattern of modern economic growth. Whether this part of the theory, dealing with qualifications and modifications of the general pattern of modern economic growth, or still better with the important *classes* of deviations from that pattern, should be extended into the range where the initial structures are so unfavorable as to inhibit modern economic growth, remains to be seen. Even without such an extension, the model of the common features of the industrial system and its social concomitants, combined with the analysis of the major modifications due to diverse initial structures of even the developed nations, would suggest reasons for the failure of other nations to adopt the industrial system successfully.

c) The third indispensable part of the theory would be aimed at a model dealing with the pattern and mechanism of the spread of the industrial system throughout the world. A major epochal innovation of this type could, abstractly speaking, originate in all parts of the world simultaneously and affect at the same time and with the same intensity all the units within the world community. Given the diversity in structure of the different parts of the world at any one time, however, such an occurrence is highly unlikely since only some units are ready to originate or adopt it simultaneously. In fact, the industrial system, like the mercantile system and other major innovations marking off whole historical epochs, originated in one part of the world, and then spread first to the major follower countries (e.g., the United States and Germany, which followed Great Britain as the pioneer); then to the next set of countries, among which Japan was prominent; and more recently to the U.S.S.R.

The basic mechanism of inter-action among nations, characterized by diverse structures and affected by the unequal impact of modern economic growth spreading from one country to another, and the elements of some comprehensible order in the sequential spread of the industrial system, are the two major topics of this part of the theory of economic growth. Much raw material for the former is contained in the vast literature on international trade, international capital movements, international migration, colonialism and imperialism, and war—to name but a few fields. At present, this is only raw material that has yet to be integrated into a cogent model of the mechanism of inter-action among nations in all its important aspects. The raw material for the theory of the sequential spread lies in the comparative analysis of the characteristics of the successive follower countries, and some benefit might ensue from a comparison of these aspects with those of the spread of some earlier epochal innovations. To be sure, some general features of such a sequence are simple and obvious enough to be apparent without much analysis. For example, a major innovation will most likely spread from the country of origin to closely related and similar countries—not to distant and dissimilar countries. It follows that as the spread extends, it will reach into areas with structural characteristics increasingly different from the country of origin; the social conditions under which the industrial system will be adopted will therefore show increasing diversity and departure from the original pattern. Furthermore, the spread of an innovation means an increasing number of competitors for the pioneer or early follower countries. In a world of competing sovereign states, the friction thus generated may be aggravated as the industrial system spreads to more states with more diversified, historically-conditioned social and political structures. But all these are rather plausible conjectures, glimpses of elements of order, that would have to be pursued much further in systematic theory-oriented analysis.

d) The three tasks of theory, distinguished above, are clearly interrelated; in any account of the comparative growth of nations all of them have to be performed. The common features of modern economic growth cannot be firmly established and analyzed unless the divergent features are also recognized and associated with the factors that determine them. The theory of the sequential spread and of the mechanism of inter-action among nations will necessarily yield another set of factors producing differences in patterns of growth among nations—the pioneers and the followers, the first and second sets of followers, and so on—and thus will contribute to the second part of the theory, as well as to the dynamics of the industrial system itself.

Yet the distinction is significant because it separates the general model of the internal pattern of modern economic growth of a country from the modifications of such a pattern by structural characteristics such as size, resources, etc., and because it separates the model of a nation's modern economic growth from the model of the international spread of the industrial system. Such separation is useful since it permits us to see upon what part of the whole corpus of theory the various findings and data have bearing. Thus, we are able to perceive more clearly than we otherwise could the gaps and the lines of further inquiry and analysis.

KNOWLEDGE AND POLICY

The theoretical orientation discussed in the preceding section indicates goals of inquiry that are ambitious and far-flung. It may justifiably be asked whether study so oriented can ever reach such goals, and if it cannot, whether it is likely to be of much value for uses by which all knowledge ought to be tested, that is, in application to policy problems. Presumably it is in such application— the implicit or explicit prediction of the consequences of alternative policies or disturbances—that the validity and usefulness of theoretical analysis and empirical findings are tested. This seems to be particularly true in the field of economic growth which has emerged to almost fashionable prominence in recent years because growth problems in developed, underdeveloped, and still developing countries have been pressing for solution.

I raise this broad question hesitantly, partly because it cannot be treated effectively in a few paragraphs, partly because I am naturally reluctant to spend the time and effort that could be devoted to substantive matters on methodological questions which can be truly tested only in active research, and the general answers to which must necessarily be articles of faith to be taken on faith. Yet, at times, in some areas of analysis, the purposes of the theoretical models and findings that pile up must be explicitly considered. Otherwise, some implicit and poorly-prepared answers may well contain a dangerous misconception of the full range of true relations between knowledge and policy, leading to a mis-application of findings and to a wasteful allocation of intellectual and other resources in the field of inquiry. The tentative answers given below naturally reflect my own thinking and approach; stating them explicitly may at least have the value of inducing other students in the field also to deal overtly with these questions.

My answer to the broad question raised above can be set down in three general propositions. First, let us assume that the ambitious theoretical goals are forever beyond reach; that the supply of empirical data and resources that can be devoted to their analysis will forever fall short of requirements for resolving the problems set by the complexity of the process in which we are attempting to establish a testable intellectual order. This does not mean that the findings made *on the way* to these unattainable goals, the partial generalizations, the few elements of order that will be found, are not valuable contributions to tested knowledge—even though they are yet to be incorporated into a wider over-all scheme, and the tests are, therefore, not complete. We should learn to accept and recognize the limited character of partial generalizations. Otherwise, *unless* a broad conception of the interrelated theoretical goals and of the variety of experience that must be included is kept in mind, there is the grave danger that the parts of the process that can be more easily generalized will be taken out of their limiting context and made the subject of some theoretical model or empirical generalization for which unwarranted validity will be claimed. We have had a number of such generalizations in the history of economics, in which trends or relations suggested by a limited segment of historical experience have been extrapolated far beyond their legitimate empirical base. Consequently, many have proved to be wrong. The projections of long-term economic growth made by the Classical and Marxian schools are illustrations that come easily to mind; so do such purely empirical generalizations as Pareto's "laws" of the size-distribution of incomes.

Second, to assume that the major use of ordered and tested knowledge lies in its application to specific policy problems, is far too narrow a conception. In the social science fields, in particular, the foremost aim of ordered knowledge is to enrich the direct experience of current generations with those of the past, and to widen the horizon of experience of a given nation by the experience of others. The value of such an enriched and widened background of ordered knowledge, i.e., one related to various patterns of condition and adaptation, lies, of course, in making responses more intelligent and less susceptible to narrow attitudes that often treat current events and problems as completely new and view a nation's customary patterns and values as the only ones to be considered. Obviously, such use of wider knowledge as a prerequisite for, and inducement to, more carefully considered attitudes towards events and problems, also involves implicit projection: it means comparisons of the present with the past, of a given nation's experience and values with those of another, and both of these with the expectation that analogous and different situations will lead to analogous and different results. This is a far cry from using highly determinate and hence narrowly geared models and generalizations for the estimation of probable effects of specifically defined, alternate policies of action on a given problem.

The *practical* value of the wider perspective of knowledge, transcending narrow national and time boundaries, for an intelligent and effective response to problems posed by economic growth, can hardly be exaggerated. For such knowledge, if shared by decision-making groups in society, will limit the chance of narrow, parochial, and dogmatic answers. And such a contribution in terms of any measurable purely material effect, is far greater than the presumptive contribution of narrowly conceived economic predictions of alternative handling of specific policy questions. The former should affect the whole climate in which basic decisions are made and the sense of vision that will guide them; the latter are tools, useful to be sure, but only tools geared to perform specific assignments. The difference in effect has no true analogy in the natural sciences; but its magnitude may be likened to that between theoretical physics and a branch of engineering.

Third, the kind of theoretical orientation we are suggesting should perform an essential destructive function already hinted at above. Because economists have been called upon to provide hard and fast answers to current problems and to do so even though such answers are not warranted by the state of knowledge, there has been a tendency to overcome the limitation of available empirical knowledge by inferences from principles which, in the context of the times and the given civilization, seem plausible. The resulting overgeneralization and dogmatism have made economics an effective weapon in social policy but unfortunately they have also made of the corpus of economic theory a series of generalizations of decreasing validity, of increasing sophistication, but also of increasingly uncertain applicability, and of non-resolved contradictions that on the surface seem to be purely conceptual but are at bottom related to divergent social positions and different policy implications. The prolonged survival of generalizations far beyond their usefulness as tools of understanding and social progress is one example of cultural lag in which social experience abounds. Some reasons for this survival, e.g., the vested interests of social groups, parties, nations, classes, are beyond our concern here. However, if such survival is encouraged by the view that a theory, no matter how partial or obsolete, is to be preserved because it gives determinate answers, and can be killed off only by an alternative, equally determinate theory, it may be hoped that orientation to a broader theoretical framework, the cumulative weight of ordered evidence produced by such orientation, and a wider conception of the relation between knowledge and policy, would serve to destroy dangerously obsolete theories that have become enshrined in national or class myths. This would be an immediate service—at least to the intellectual workers in the field, and perhaps, after a time, to the decision-making groups.

One final observation can be made. An explicitly wide theoretical orientation in which the intellectual structure is relevant to a broad variety of national and historical experience, also necessarily emphasizes the factual foundation—particularly the evidence that can be put into definite forms, detached from intuitive, direct perception. For with such a wide framework, no theorist could rely on the unorganized knowledge that he may have of his own country and epoch, nor could he entertain the hope that his imagination, exercised in spinning out inferences, could even approach the variety of experience encountered even in a first approximate review of empirical evidence. It is the resulting emphasis on the primacy of empirical evidence which lends this wide theoretical orientation the promise of cumulative additions to valuable generalizations and findings; which strengthens the prospect that the knowledge thus derived will lead toward a more intelligent response to major problems of economic growth; and which encourages the hope that it will mitigate, if not completely dissolve, the variety of dogmatic viewpoints that are survivals of past overgeneralizations no longer useful as tools for understanding or for social policy.